catching
readers

grade 2

THE RESEARCH-INFORMED CLASSROOM SERIES

Consider daily life for a child struggling with reading. Imagine what it is like to go through school day after day feeling that you are bad at the one thing that school seems to value most. Imagine struggling with everything from independent reading to reading directions on a math worksheet. Imagine what that feels like. . . .

While there are all sorts of pressures to improve instruction for struggling readers—to raise test scores, to make adequate yearly progress (AYP), and so on—the most compelling reason is to help as many children as possible avoid that feeling. We want to enable children to go through elementary school feeling, and being, successful.

Barbara Taylor brings decades of research and development to the question of how to help struggling readers become successful. *Catching Readers: Grade 2*, which is part of the Early Intervention in Reading series, brings the resulting insights to you, in the form of concrete and specific practices that have been shown to help children who struggle to improve their reading. These books could not come at a more important time, as response to intervention (RTI) leads schools to invest more than ever in small-group reading instruction. The multifaceted and responsive teaching at the heart of the approach Taylor describes is a welcome contrast to the myopic, scripted programs marketed so heavily under the banner of RTI.

These books exemplify the ideals of the Research-Informed Classroom series—bringing rigorous classroom-based research to bear on persistent challenges of classroom practice. This series aims to bridge the gap between research and practice by focusing on the most practical, classroom-relevant research and communicating practices based on that research in a way that makes them accessible, appealing, and actionable. The series is founded on the belief that students and teachers are researchers' clients, and serving them should be the highest priority.

As with so much of the best educational research and development, Taylor has collaborated extensively with teachers close to home and throughout the United States. Indeed, one might say we've gone full circle, from Teacher-Informed Research to Research-Informed Teaching. So thank you, teachers, and thank you, Barbara, for this important contribution to reading success for all children.

—*Nell K. Duke*

MICHIGAN STATE UNIVERSITY

catching
readers

grade 2

DAY-BY-DAY SMALL-GROUP READING INTERVENTIONS

Barbara M. Taylor

HEINEMANN
Portsmouth, NH

Heinemann
361 Hanover Street
Portsmouth, NH 03801–3912
www.heinemann.com

Offices and agents throughout the world

The author and publisher wish to thank those who have generously given permission to reprint borrowed material in this book and/or on the DVD:

Cover art and excerpt from *Five Silly Fishermen* by Roberta Edwards, illustrated by Sylvie Wickstrom. Text copyright © 1989 by Random House, Inc. Illustrations copyright © 1989 by Sylvie Wickstrom. Used by permission of Random House Children's Books, a division of Random House, Inc.
For on-line information about other Random House, Inc. books and authors, see the Internet website at http://www.randomhouse.com.

Cover art from *The Happy Day* by Ruth Krauss. Illustrations copyright © 1949 by Marc Simont. Copyright © renewed 1977 by Marc Simont. Used by permission of HarperCollins Publishers.

Cover art from *Four on the Shore: Level Three* by Edward Marshall, illustrated by James Marshall. Text copyright © 1985 by Edward Marshall. Illustrations copyright © 1985 by James Marshall. Published by Penguin Group (USA) Inc. Books for Young Readers. Used by permission of the publisher.

Library of Congress Cataloging-in-Publication Data
Taylor, Barbara M.
  Catching readers, grade 2 : day-by-day small-group reading interventions / Barbara M. Taylor.
    p. cm.—(Early intervention in reading series) (The research-informed classroom series)
  Includes bibliographical references.
  ISBN-13: 978-0-325-02889-7
  ISBN-10: 0-325-02889-3
  1. Language arts (Primary). 2. Reading (Primary). 3. English language—Composition and exercises—Study and teaching (Primary). 4. Communication in small groups. I. Title.
  LB1528.T37 2010
  372.41'62—dc22   2010007138

Editor: Wendy Murray
Production editor: Patricia Adams
Video editor: Sherry Day
Video producer: Bob Schuster, Real Productions
Cover design: Lisa Fowler
Typesetter: Gina Poirier Design
Manufacturing: Valerie Cooper

Printed in the United States of America on acid-free paper
14 13 12 11 10 ML 1 2 3 4 5

This book is dedicated to the many
second-grade teachers who work tirelessly
to provide motivating instruction that meets
their students' needs, challenges them all,
and is instrumental to their success in reading.

Contents

1 Helping Second Graders Who Struggle
Lessons That Sit Within Effective Reading Instruction **1**

2 Meet the Teachers
The Differentiated Lessons and Teacher
Collaboration That Support EIR **19**

On the DVD

See-It-in-Action Video Clips

Downloadable Classroom Reproducibles

Over 100 pages of full-size forms and teaching resources.

Teaching Resources on the DVD

Foreword

I began my teaching career as a first-grade teacher in Key West, Florida, in 1965. Much has changed since then in the world and in the world of school. But reading Barbara Taylor's books made me realize how much is still the same. My class of thirty-five children contained nine children—two girls and seven boys—who were (in the lingo of the day) "not ready." In those days, basal reading series for first grade had a readiness book that I was very grateful to find. I grouped these nine students together and we made our way through the workbook pages. The pages were mostly practice with letter names and auditory discrimination—the precursor of phonemic awareness. Six weeks into the school year, we finished the readiness book and I administered the Metropolitan Readiness Test to my students. For three days, I tried to keep them focused on the correct lines and asked them to underline the letter *b*, put an *x* on the picture that began like *paint,* and circle the picture of the object that rhymed with *cat*. I took all these booklets home and spent a miserable weekend grading them. As I made my way through the test booklets, I adopted a "benefit of the doubt" scoring system. "Two red marks on this line, none on the next. If the second mark is on the next line, it would be right. I'm counting it correct." In spite of my lenient scoring, scores for eight of the nine children indicated they were still "not ready." I spent a sleepless Sunday night wondering what I was to do with these children who were clearly not ready when I had used up all the readiness materials! Lacking any alternative, I started them in the first pre-primer and we plodded our way through the books. By the end of the year, only one of these students could read fluently at primer level.

If Barbara had written her books 45 years earlier (when she was probably in kindergarten), I think I could have transformed my "not ready" kids into fluent readers. Based on many years of research in real classrooms with real teachers and kids, Barbara has created a workable system for providing struggling readers in grades K–5 with the targeted intervention they need to become fluent readers. At the heart of Early Intervention in Reading (EIR) is the addition of a second reading lesson in a small-group setting. Unlike many interventions, struggling readers get this second reading lesson *in addition to* all the rich classroom instruction and *in* the classroom—not in some room down the hall. With details, specifics, and examples that only someone who has spent many hours in the classroom could know, Barbara guides you step-by-step as you organize for and provide effective EIR instruction. As you read through the book, your brain races with questions:

- "How do I fit an additional intervention group lesson into my daily schedule?"

- "What books work best for these lessons?"

- "How can I provide all the instruction struggling readers need in 20 minutes?"

- "What does the coaching for decoding and comprehension look like and sound like?"

- "How do I wean them off my coaching and move them toward independence?"

- "How do I provide worthwhile independent activities for the students I am not working with?"

Because Barbara has worked in many so classrooms coaching teachers who are implementing EIR, she can provide practical, classroom-tested answers to all your questions. She invites you into the classrooms of real teachers and you get to hear them describing how they organize and problem solve. In addition to the printed resource, you can go to the video clips on the DVD to "See It in Action." As you watch real teachers move through the three-day lesson sequence, you realize that, while it is complex, Barbara provides all the resources you need to make it work in your classrooms with your students who struggle.

Once you see how EIR works in your classroom, you will probably want to spread the word. Not to worry! Barbara is right there supporting you. In the final chapter, "Creating an EIR Community," she provides a detailed, month-by-month plan for organizing a group of colleagues to learn together how to better meet the needs of struggling readers.

So, if they ever invent a time machine that could transport me back to 1965, with the help of Barbara Taylor's books, I know I could teach all my "not ready" kids to read!

Patricia M. Cunningham
Wake Forest University

Acknowledgments

● ●

This book is the result of twenty years of collaboration with many second-grade teachers and colleagues across the United States. I want to thank them all for their invaluable contributions to this book.

Inspired by Reading Recovery, I developed the Early Intervention in Reading (EIR) process in the late 1980s to help first-grade teachers help their at-risk readers succeed in reading through daily, small-group intervention lessons. I have refined the EIR process over the years by visiting many classrooms and working with and learning from many teachers and their students. Without this opportunity, I would not have been able to modify and improve the EIR teaching strategies and professional learning practices described in this book.

I also want to thank the hundreds of teachers I have visited and learned from over the past ten years through my work on effective reading instruction and school-wide reading improvement. I especially want to thank the exemplary second-grade teachers who have contributed so much to this book by sharing their thoughts and effective reading lessons.

I owe a special thanks and a debt of gratitude to my colleague, Ceil Critchley, a master teacher who has helped teachers succeed with EIR through the phenomenal professional learning support she has provided to them over many years. Without Ceil's expert guidance, teachers would not have been as successful as they have been in helping their at-risk readers learn to read well by the end of the year.

I also want to recognize my academic colleagues for their support and feedback. In particular, thanks to my good friends, Kathy Au and Taffy Raphael, for gently nudging me over the years to publish my work on EIR in a form readily accessible to teachers.

I want to thank the many people at Heinemann who have made this book possible. First, thanks to Wendy Murray, my editor, who saw the value of this book for teachers with its focus on an instructional process, not materials and a script to follow, for at-risk readers. She has done a remarkable job cutting unnecessary chunks, adding teacher-friendly phrases, reorganizing entire sections, and designing the book so it is easy for teachers to read and use. I also want to thank Patty Adams, my production editor, for her top-notch work on a complex project within a challenging time frame. Whenever I called with questions or concerns, she responded cheerfully and promptly. Many others at Heinemann have also contributed to this book and I thank them for their efforts.

It is my sincere hope that second-grade teachers will find this book useful as they strive to teach students who are a little behind in the fall to be confident, successful readers by the end of the school year. Thanks to all the teachers for the important work you do for our children!

Barbara M. Taylor
University of Minnesota

Introduction

W̲e are a culture of quick fixes. We promise mastery in ten easy lessons, instant success, overnight sensations. Go to a bookstore and whether you stand and gaze at the brightly colored covers in the business, health, or education section, the answer to our every need is couched in words like *speedy, easy*, and *seven easy steps*.

In such a culture alarm bells go off when a teacher faces a seven-year-old child in second grade who is behind in learning to read. *Catching Readers, Grade 2,* is one book in a series of five. This book is dedicated to giving the regular classroom teacher what's needed to reach and teach that seven-year-old. Early Intervention in Reading is a concrete plan rather than a frantic pull-out program or a misguided label. Each book in the series offers teacher-friendly, research-proven background and lessons for young readers who need an extra boost.

The intervention model brings reading success to children in a three-day lesson cycle, which I know sounds as though I'm playing into the same glib promises of swift solutions. I state it here as a way to express that it is a three-day format used across a school year with deep roots—more than twenty years of classroom testing. I emphasize the "three-day" repetition of the lessons to make it clear that we don't have to choose to run around in circles looking for some new complicated program for reaching at-risk readers. We know what to do. When we're true to children's developmental levels, know which books to put in their hands, and provide effective instruction, a lot of good things fall into place. The key is to focus on the children and the practices we know help them to read at each grade level.

In fact, the intervention model I offer stands in opposition to approaches and programs that think the answer to helping K–5 below-grade-level readers achieve is to provide remediation. Above-grade-level, on-grade-level, and below-grade-level readers all need the same thing: sound teaching techniques and developmentally appropriate practices that meet their needs and provide intellectual challenge to all.

Here's an overview of how the interventions are unique and yet similar for each grade level, so you can see the developmentally based, purposeful overlap in the series. The intervention gives teachers, staff developers, principals, and reading coaches a predictable model so that schoolwide coherence is easier to attain. All grade-level models stress word recognition proficiency, high-level comprehension, vocabulary development, and strategic reading. Unique components of the various grade-specific models are described below:

Kindergarten

The daily 10-minute supplemental lessons for kindergarten focus on developing all children's oral language, phonemic awareness, and emergent literacy abilities through literature-based activities. The goal is for all students to leave kindergarten with the skills they need to learn to read in first grade. The more capable children, as they respond to the various activities in EIR lessons, serve as models for the children who are less skilled in oral language and emergent literacy abilities. Less-skilled children who need more support return to some of the story discussion questions and phonemic awareness/emergent literacy activities for an additional 10 minutes a day.

First Grade

First-grade children who start the school year with lower-than-average phonemic awareness abilities and letter–sound knowledge will benefit from EIR lessons. The teacher focuses on accelerating students' literacy learning by deliberately coaching them to use strategies to decode words and to think at a higher level about the meaning of the texts they are reading.

Second Grade

Second-grade readers who can't read a book at a first-grade level at the start of second grade will benefit from the basic EIR routine. The intervention begins with first-grade books and routines of the grade 1 EIR model and then moves into second-grade books a few months later. There is also an accelerated grade 2 routine designed for students who come to second grade as independent readers but who will need additional support to be reading on grade level by the end of the school year.

Third Grade

The grade 3 EIR routine is for children who are reading below grade level when they enter third grade. In the grade 3 EIR model, the focus is on refining students' decoding of multisyllabic words, improving their fluency, developing their vocabulary, and enhancing their comprehension of narrative and informational texts. Ideally, the grade 3 EIR model is done within the context of a cross-age tutoring program in which the third-grade students read to and also tutor first-grade EIR students. The third graders are working on their reading for more than "catching up because they are behind." They look forward to and enjoy working with their younger student who needs additional support in reading.

Fourth/Fifth

The EIR routine for fourth and fifth grade is for children who are reading below grade level at the beginning of the school year. Although students receive support in attacking multisyllabic words and developing reading fluency, the grade 4/5 model focuses on improving students' comprehension of informational text through the use of comprehension strategies, discussion of vocabulary, and engagement in high-level talk and writing about texts. Ideally, the grade 4/5 EIR model is done within the context of a motivating cross-age tutoring program in which fourth and fifth graders read to and also tutor second or third graders.

Getting Good at It: Different Ways to Use This Book

This book—and by extension all the books in this series—is designed to be used by the individual teacher, a pair or group of teachers, or as part of a schoolwide professional development plan. Here are components that support collaborative learning:

Video Clips for Individual Viewing

As you read about the recurring cycle of EIR routines, I encourage you to watch the video clips that illustrate what is being covered in the text. Many teachers have told me that seeing the EIR routines being applied in the classroom makes it easy to start teaching the EIR lessons. See this icon throughout the book for easy access to the video clips and teaching resources on the DVD.

Guidance for Monthly Sessions with Colleagues

In the last chapter, "Creating an EIR Community," I share a model for a professional learning community (PLC) that works. Over my many years of working with teachers on effective reading instruction generally, and EIR lessons specifically, I have learned from teachers' comments that the collaborative nature of learning new instructional techniques with colleagues leads to excellent understanding, reflection, and success.

Website Support

For additional support, go to www.Heinemann.com and search by Taylor or *Catching Readers* for answers to questions that will likely arise about teaching EIR lessons. Also, see the Heinemann website to learn more about the availability of additional support from an EIR expert and consulting support.

We can help so many children become successful readers when we offer excellent reading instruction and provide effective interventions to those students who require additional reading support within their classroom setting. I am excited to have the opportunity to offer my *Catching Readers* series of books to you. Thank you for the important work you do for our children!

Helping Second Graders Who Struggle

. . . .

Lessons That Sit Within Effective Reading Instruction

S econd graders' growth in reading is amazing. Most students come to your classroom in the fall as beginning readers who read short texts with controlled vocabularies. By May, most students are reading chapter books with fluency and expression. However, the range of students' reading abilities is great. In the fall, some students read fluently, many still read haltingly, and some cannot yet read. This book and the companion video clips and teacher resources on the DVD are aimed at helping teachers arrive at this level of effectiveness sooner to reach those students who struggle with reading.

My career as a researcher and teacher educator has been dedicated to studying and describing components of effective literacy instruction so that teachers can become more intentional in their teaching and more confident in their interactions with children around all aspects of reading instruction. Through this book, my goal is for you to gain a comfort level teaching small-group reading lessons for young children who struggle with reading, but I also show you how this intervention work connects to and informs all the rich literacy practices that occur within a balanced literacy framework. When you learn how to teach reading to struggling readers well, I've found it makes you a more effective reading teacher all around.

How the Early Intervention in Reading Model Sits Within Effective Reading Instruction

The small-group intervention lessons featured in this book are based on Early Intervention in Reading (EIR®), a set of teaching practices I developed that incorporates the characteristics of effective reading instruction (see page 3). It's been in practice for twenty years in schools, and if you're a teacher looking to implement Response to Intervention (RTI) or differentiated instruction, you'll see that my model can easily be used to meet these current calls to action. EIR provides:

▶ second-graders who struggle to read an additional daily opportunity to interact with text in a structured, consistent, and comfortable small-group setting

▶ second-grade teachers with a repetitive, clear structure that helps them support these children so they can catch up or keep up with grade-level expectations for reading

▶ teachers and schools an intervention model that isn't stigmatizing for children because it uses authentic literature and practices, and is done within the regular classroom—and usually by the classroom teacher

I want to emphasize that I developed this model with classroom teachers in mind—based on my belief that students shouldn't be pulled out of the classroom for extra help. Rather, teachers need to learn to support them during the reading block. They also need to harness the collective power of colleagues and work together to help all children learn to read well. Supplemental instruction for those who are struggling can't be something that only the special teachers of reading know about.

Through structured, 20-minute lessons, a group of struggling readers are provided with an extra shot of daily quality reading instruction. A regular classroom teacher supports and coaches individual students based on need, so it accelerates students' reading progress. The structure adapts around midyear to children's development as readers, and because it has been refined after decades of research and practice, it's a model that teachers are less likely to abandon or use inconsistently. They see their students making striking gains in

How EIR Meets the Requirements of Effective Reading Instruction

	Effective Reading Instruction	EIR Lessons
What You Teach (Content)	Explicit phonemic awareness instruction	Sound boxes, writing for sounds in sentence writing
	Systematic phonics instruction	Scope and sequence, making words, writing for sounds in sentence writing, coaching in word-recognition strategies
	Oral reading for fluency	Repeated reading of stories, coached reading with feedback, one-on-one reading with aide or volunteer
	Text-based vocabulary instruction	Discussion of word meanings at point of contact in EIR stories
	Comprehension strategies instruction	Summarizing stories, practicing comprehension monitoring
	Comprehension instruction in the context high-level talk about text	Coaching for high-level comprehension through questioning
How You Teach (Pedagogy)	Application of taught skills and strategies to text	Applying taught skills and strategies to text
	Differentiated instruction	Support is provided by teacher to individual students based on need
	Balance of direct teaching and providing support	Coaching students to use taught skills and strategies as they read EIR stories
	Teaching with clear purpose and good timing	Stating teaching purposes routinely, covering daily steps of each 20-minute lesson at a rapid pace
	Active student engagement	All students read, write, talk, share with a partner, engage in word work
	Student engagement in challenging, motivating learning activities	Students read just-right stories that require them to "glue to the print" from the beginning, spend only three days on a story, and move on to new challenges with a new text. EIR stories that are selected are engaging texts.
	Developing independent learners	High expectations, releasing to students, partner work
	Motivating classroom	Using praise, helpful feedback, demonstrating enthusiasm for learning
Professional Learning	Collaborative learning with a focus on practice	Monthly learning meetings to discuss EIR strategies, successes, and challenges

their reading, which makes it highly motivating. Later in this chapter and in Chapter 3, we'll look at the three-day lesson cycle in detail, but here is a glimpse of how these lessons extend and amplify the effective reading instruction you do with all of your students.

Which Children Need the Intervention and What's the End Goal?

Students who benefit from the EIR lessons that are described in Chapter 3 are those who come to second grade not yet reading first-grade texts independently. Without solid intervention lessons, these children are likely to fail to become independent readers in second grade. In Chapter 6, I describe the accelerated EIR model for students who come to second grade reading but who will need extra support to be reading on grade level by the end of the year. EIR strategies were first developed for students in grade 1 (Taylor et al. 1992) and are now developed for grades K–5. EIR is effective with many different types of regular reading programs (e.g., basal, reading and writing workshop, systematic phonics). In Chapter 7, I describe assessments you can use to determine which students might benefit from EIR.

On average, 72 percent of the children who need EIR in grade 1 are reading independently (on a primer level or higher) by May of first grade (Taylor 2001). It would be wonderful if all students are reading at an end-of-first-grade level by May. However, if struggling, emergent first-grade readers can pick up a book at the primer level that they have never seen before and read the book with at least 90 percent accuracy, most will be able to read second-grade material in second grade.

Because there are students who come to second grade not yet reading and who will need a reading intervention, I developed the grade 2 basic EIR strategies (Taylor et al. 1997). In second grade, 86 percent of the children, on average, who come to school in the fall reading at or below a primer level, are able to read on a second grade level by the end of the year if they receive grade 2 EIR lessons for the entire school year (Taylor 2001). Follow-up research demonstrates that 92 percent of these children are reading on a grade 3 level in third grade.

The basic grade 2 EIR strategies, designed for students who come to second grade not yet reading, are very similar to the grade 1 EIR strategies (Taylor 2010a). Students just move at a faster pace since they do have more reading abilities than they did in first grade, even if they are not yet independent readers. These strategies are described in detail in Chapters 3–5. For students who come to second grade as readers, but who need some support during the year to read on grade level by May, I developed the grade 2 accelerated EIR strategies. With these students, a teacher starts about halfway through the basic grade 2 model and moves into more advanced intervention strategies using end-of-grade-2 texts by the middle of the school year. This acceleration of the basic grade 2 model is described in Chapter 6.

A Brief Review of the Learning-to-Read Process

Before we turn to the specific EIR model, I want to provide a brief review of the learning-to-read process. (Also see Taylor 1998 on the DVD resources for Chapter 1.) To be most effective in helping struggling readers learn how to read, teachers need to have a clear model in their heads of what it is that children are learning how to do. Additionally, the elements discussed later tend to be the ones struggling beginning readers have the most trouble internalizing.

The Role of Phonemic Awareness in Learning to Read

Teachers hear a lot about *phonemic awareness*, or the ability to hear the sounds in words and blend those sounds together. Extensive research (Adams 1990; National Reading Panel Report [NRP] 2000; Snow, Burns, and Griffin 1998) shows that children who come to first grade with low phonemic awareness are at considerable risk of failing to learn to read in first grade.

Phonemic awareness is one of the two best predictors of end-of-first-grade reading achievement. The other good predictor is letter name knowledge. However, quickly teaching children the letter names in first grade does not have a big impact on their May reading achievement most likely because letter name knowledge serves as a proxy for the literacy environment that children have been in before they get to first grade.

Fortunately, kindergarten interventions, as well as interventions in early first grade, can make a big difference in accelerating children's phonemic awareness and hence impact their end-of-first-grade reading achievement. Phonemic awareness is an auditory ability. Segmentation of sounds, blending of sounds, hearing alliteration, and recognizing rhymes are all measures of phonemic awareness. However, the two measures most predictive of end-of-first-grade reading achievement are phoneme segmentation and blending abilities (Adams 1990; NRP 2000; Snow, Burns, and Griffin 1998). For example, a student who gives the sounds in *cat* as /c/ /a/ /t/ is segmenting the sounds. A student who blends the sounds /c/ /a/ /t/ into *cat* is blending sounds into a word.

Partial Decoding and Grasping the Alphabetic Principle

When children first try to decode words, they begin with partial decoding plus use of context. They typically start using the first letter to sound out a word but can get all the way through a word. They are also using context clues. In fact, beginning readers at first overly on context to figure out words. The arrow heading downward in Figure 1-1 represents the "aha" moment, or the time at which the light bulb goes on when children finally understand the alphabetic principle, or how to sound out words. When they get to this point, they understand that within a printed word there are letters that represent phonemes (sounds) that have to be voiced separately and blended together to make up a word. It can be hard for adults to realize just how difficult this understanding is for children to develop. But there are often a handful of children who come to first grade not knowing exactly what makes up a printed word and not knowing what the sounds are in a given word.

As adults, this seems like such a simple concept, so we think that if we explain it, children will catch on quickly. Most first-grade children grasp the alphabetic principle fairly quickly in the fall and then tend to grow very quickly in their reading abilities. Unfortunately, most children who need EIR lessons in second grade didn't grasp the alphabetic principle until April or May of first grade. In the fall, a few second-grade students may still not grasp it. This development is just a slower, gradual process for the children who need EIR and something I have come to accept over the years. As teachers, we need to be patient, believe in the children, and keep working with them. In fact, I am always impressed with the incredible patience demonstrated by the teachers I visit who are using EIR strategies with their struggling readers.

Second-grade children who are not yet reading in the fall may seem willing to give it another try since they are now a lot older than they there were in first grade, but they may give up quickly if they do not rapidly experience success with "breaking the code" in the fall. For this reason, it is very important that teachers get their EIR groups up and running no later than October.

Stages of Word-Recognition Development

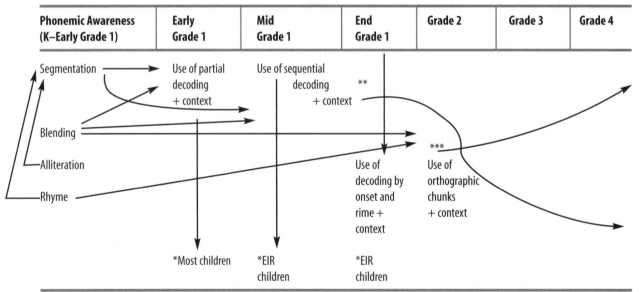

* understands alphabetic principle
** use of context falls off
*** automaticity increases

Figure 1-1 Stages of Word-Recognition Development

Learning How to Decode Letter by Letter and by Onset and Rime

EIR instructional strategies emphasize teaching children to use word-recognition strategies and to depend on themselves as they use these strategies. Letter-by-letter sequential decoding is only one strategy we teach children to use, but it is a very important strategy for them to learn in order for them to become independent readers. When children come to the word *pig*, they need to be able to sound out each letter—/p/ /i/ /g/—and blend the sounds together into *pig*. Teachers need to repeatedly model and coach children in letter-by-letter sequential decoding to help them catch on to the alphabetic principle.

Research suggests that children have to understand the concept of letter-by-letter sequential decoding before they can independently decode by onset and rime (Taylor 1998). Children can decode by onset and rime—/f/ /ind/ is *find*—when prompted to do so. However, they do not regularly use decoding by onset and rime as an independent strategy until they succeed at letter-by-letter sequential decoding.

It is also important to realize that as children start to "glue to the print" as they decode words, they begin to rely much less on context to help them figure out words. Teachers need to remind children to think about what would make sense in the story as they are sounding out words because doing so will make it easier for them to come up with the correct word.

By the end of first grade into second grade, decoding by onset and rime becomes the preferred decoding strategy for children. That is, if they recognize a chunk (e.g., phonogram), they will decode this way since it is quicker than letter-by-letter sequential decoding (Taylor 1998).

Developing Automaticity

The goal in teaching children to recognize words is that they are able to do so automatically. By second grade and into third grade, children are reading most words automatically as sight words. This doesn't mean that we have to drill on words as sight words; however, through reading for meaning, children develop automaticity for certain words by repeated exposure to these words over time.

By the time children are fully automatic in word recognition, they do not depend on context to help them recognize most words. Of course, there will be words they come across in their reading that they have never seen before, but by fourth grade most children typically read with context-free, automatic word recognition.

The Role of Comprehension and Vocabulary in Learning to Read

The purpose of reading is to gain meaning from the text, and it is important to stress both comprehension and vocabulary with emerging readers. Unfortunately, too often, especially with struggling readers, the emphasis on learning to read lies with breaking the code to the neglect of reading for meaning. Effective second-grade teachers, as we see in the lessons highlighted in Chapter 2, emphasize reading for meaning and enjoyment along with word recognition. In EIR intervention lessons, comprehension is one of four components covered every day with struggling readers.

The What and How of Good Second-Grade Teaching

My intervention model was developed with key elements of content (the what) and pedagogy (the how) as its foundation. Effective teachers tend to have good day-to-day awareness of both content and pedagogy. With that in mind, in Chapter 2 you will see lesson highlights from May Holder, Leah Davis, and Diane Swanson, teachers who represent urban, suburban, and rural settings. You'll gain a sense of how these teachers connect EIR lessons to their overall reading instruction. These three teachers not only teach EIR lessons but also provide effective reading instruction to all their students and see excellent growth in their students' reading abilities during each school year.

Content: Four Dimensions Young Readers Need

The content of excellent reading instruction has many dimensions, all of which develop the abilities students need to become competent readers. These dimensions, which are supported by a sound body of reading research, are:

▶ word-recognition development (including phonemic awareness, phonics)

▶ fluency development

▶ vocabulary development

▶ comprehension development

Do they comprise a complete universe of what leads children to become successful, engaged readers? No, but these are the nonnegotiable aspects of teaching reading in second grade. Without them, all the other practices won't have a sufficient foundation on which to build successful readers.

Word-Recognition Development

Most students, especially those in kindergarten and early first grade, benefit from systematic, explicit instruction in phonemic awareness that focuses on hearing the sounds in words and blending these sounds into words (Adams 1990; NRP 2000; Snow, Burns, and Griffin 1998). By second grade, even students who are struggling with reading will have fairly well-developed phonemic awareness if this has been taught in kindergarten in first grade. Thus, little phonemic awareness instruction should be needed in second grade.

A variety of approaches to systematic phonics instruction is effective (Christensen and Bowey 2005; Juel and Minden-Cupp 2000: Mathes et al. 2005; NRP 2000), including letter-by-letter decoding and decoding by onset and rime. For example, Leah's phonics instruction with average readers focuses on Making Words to reinforce their knowledge of vowel teams such as *ay*, *ai*, and *ea*.

Coaching students to use word-recognition strategies as they read stories and informational texts is another important aspect of decoding instruction. For example, when Diane is reading with a group of below-average readers and they get stuck on *swing*, she coaches them to use the chunk *ing* and the beginning /sw/ sound to come up with the word. They continue to read and come to the word *break*. Diane says, "Twisting the vowel sounds, or coming up with another sound for the vowels, is a strategy you can use to help you sound out words. If we try the long *e* sound in this word and it doesn't make sense, we can try the short *e* sound or the long *a* sound." The group sounds out the word correctly.

Fluency Development

Oral reading procedures to develop word recognition fluency, in which students receive guidance or support, also have a significant impact on students' reading (Kuhn and Stahl 2003; NRP 2000). Procedures to build fluency include repeated reading and coached reading. May Holder effectively includes fluency practice as one part of a small-group lesson with average readers. She says, "I want you to reread the story, 'Lots of Legs.' Why do good readers reread?" Students answer, "We get better at reading. So we remember it." May restates to clarify. "Yes, you get more fluent and you remember more of what you've read, don't you. Let's reread a few pages at a time, and then I'll ask you some questions to discuss with a partner." At then end, they discuss the main ideas of the article about insects.

Vocabulary Development

When it comes to developing students' vocabulary, using a variety of instructional approaches is critical, including direct instruction in specific words, pre-reading instruction in words, learning to use strategies to determine word meanings, and learning of words in rich contexts and incidentally through wide reading (Baumann and Kame'enui 2004; Blachowicz and Fisher 2000; Graves 2007; NRP 2000). Words studied should generally be those the learner will find useful in many contexts (Beck, McKeown, and Kucan 2002).

Some words need to be introduced before reading so students are not confused about a major aspect of a story. Beck and colleagues (2002) stress the value of teaching many word meanings at point of contact in the text as well as covering some words after reading when students have the benefit of context to help them understand the meanings of new words. Before Leah reads a story about Ruby Bridges to her class, they discuss the meaning of the word *equality*. As they read, she stops at the word *segregation* and tells students the meaning of the word. After reading, they return to *equality* and discuss *courageous*, *patient*, and *hopeful*, which are characteristics of Ruby Bridges.

As teachers, we have a tendency to teach more vocabulary than perhaps we should before reading and not enough at point of contact in the reading selection. On pages 24–34 you will read lessons of May, Leah, and Diane in which they provide examples of teaching important vocabulary at point of contact in the stories they are reading with their students.

Developing students' curiosity about words is also important. You can model this interest in word meanings and enthusiasm for authors' word choice in a variety of ways, and it's a boon to students' reading and writing. For example, May Holder has "Sticky Note Wednesday," which focuses on words the students have found in books at home or at schools. They write a word and the sentence in which they found it, as well as a definition if possible, on a sticky note, and they put this on a whiteboard to share with others. May also has students find what she calls "dazzling words" from the text they read together at school for the word wall to enrich students' vocabulary and to encourage them to be interested in the words around them.

Comprehension Development

Skilled readers use strategies as they read to enhance their comprehension. Also, instruction in comprehension strategies improves students' reading comprehension abilities (Foorman et al. 2006; Guthrie, Wigfield, and VonSecker 2000; NRP 2000; Pressley 2006). Explicit lessons in the following strategies are most effective: summarizing; comprehension monitoring; use of graphic and semantic organizers before, during, and after reading; use of story structure; and question answering and question generation (NRP 2000). Also, using multiple strategies, like reciprocal teaching, in naturalistic contexts, is important in terms of enhancing reading comprehension (Guthrie et al. 2004; Klingner et al. 2004; NRP 2000; Pressley 2006). The classroom examples provided on pages 24–34 exemplify instruction in comprehension strategies, including reciprocal teaching, asking and answering questions, activating background knowledge and making connections, comprehension monitoring, summarizing a story, and summarizing information text.

Teaching students how to engage in high-level talk and writing about text is another important aspect of comprehension instruction repeatedly found to be related to reading gains (Knapp 1995; Saunders and Goldenberg 1999; Taylor et al. 2003; Van den Branden 2000). High-level questions cause the students to pause and think about the text before answering. These questions expand students' comprehension of the text as they interpret it at a high level or make connections between the text and their own background knowledge and understandings of a concept. (Coaching for high-level talk about text is covered in detail in Chapter 3. See Figure 3-2 on page 47 for coaching examples of questions and prompts.) For example, after reading the story about Ruby Bridges, Leah has her students sit by one of the posters that is hanging in the room—labeled *courageous*, *patient*, and *hopeful*—that they think best describes Ruby Bridges and discuss with others by the same poster why they chose that particular word. Then, they are to go to their seats and write in their journals about which of the three characteristics of Ruby Bridges they would choose for themselves and why. Later in the chapter, there are more examples of our three teachers engaging students in high-level thinking and substantive book discussions in their lessons.

Pedagogy: The Art of Teaching Demystified

You know good teaching when you see it, and yet it can be hard to capture all the nuances of it in the confines of a book. In short, good teaching consists of all the teacher's routines and practices, as well as his or her ability to respond in the moment to students' needs and to connect to students so they feel motivated to learn. For example, techniques like clearly stating lesson purposes or offering impromptu coaching, as well as decisions that need to be made about elements such as timing (e.g., how long to spend on a particular aspect of a lesson) or what texts and tasks to use to engage students in purposeful learning activities are all parts of good teaching practices. Teachers who put effective pedagogy into practice:

▶ Strike a good balance between whole-group and small-group instruction (Chorzempa and Graham 2006)

▶ Consider the purposes and timing of lessons relative to their students' varying instructional needs

▶ Balance direct teaching (telling, leading) with providing support (e.g., coaching providing feedback) as students are engaged in learning activities (Connor, Morrison, and Katch 2004; Pressley et al. 2003; Taylor et al. 2003)

▶ Foster students' active involvement in learning activities to enhance their learning and motivation (Guthrie, Wigfield, and VonSecker 2000)

▶ Provide students with challenging, motivating activities as they are working with the teacher, on their own, or with other students (Pressley et al. 2003)

▶ Sustain culturally responsive instruction, which involves teachers building on students' cultural strengths as they structure student interactions and as they use multicultural literature that celebrates students' cultural heritages and introduces students to new cultural perspectives (Au 2006)

▶ Maintain a balanced approach to instruction that involves direct teaching of reading skills and strategies as well as giving students opportunities to apply skills and strategies to engaging texts through reading, writing, and discussing (Pressley 2006)

▶ Continually assess students' engagement, understanding, and behavior throughout the day (Pressley et al. 2003)

▶ Systematically collect and share with colleagues a variety of formal and informal student assessment data to help them make instructional decisions to improve student performance (Lipson et al. 2004; Taylor, Pearson, Clark, and Walpole 2000)

Teachers need to plan for and coordinate these many different components of second graders' learning activities during their daily 90- to 120-minute reading block.

Affective Dimensions: What It Means to Be Motivating to Kids

Another important aspect of pedagogy includes the "people skills" involved in teaching. Research and our own experiences have a lot to tell us about the impact of teachers' management, expectations, and beliefs about children on their achievement and motivation. As you read the list that follows, think about your second-grade students and how you view yourself on these aspects of effective teaching. Effective teachers in the elementary grades:

▶ Have positive classroom atmospheres and teach with enthusiasm for learning (Dolezal et al. 2003; Pressley et al. 2003)

▶ Expertly manage and organize their classrooms (Dolezal et al. 2003; Pressley 2001; Taylor, Pressley, and Pearson 2002)

▶ Provide encouragement and praise as well as positive feedback (Pressley 2006)

▶ Have high expectations for their students, communicate to students that effort leads to success, encourage independence and responsibility, provide for student choice, and foster cooperative learning experiences (Bohn, Roehrig, and Pressley 2004; Dolezal et al. 2003; Guthrie et al. 2004; Hamre and Pianta 2005; Pressley et al. 2003)

▶ Collaborate with colleagues. While individual teachers can positively improve their reading instruction and thus the development of their students' reading, it is often helpful to work with colleagues as you embark on the journey of being the most effective teacher you can be.

Having a good grasp of the content and pedagogy of effective reading instruction will inform your practice and support you in the many decisions you need to make in your day-to-day reading lessons. In turn, effective practices help your students develop into motivated, competent readers.

A Three-Day Cycle of Supplemental Instruction

Now that we have briefly reviewed effective reading instruction for all students, let's look at the EIR model, one approach to effective instruction for readers who need additional support. The EIR model, like most other successful early intervention models (e.g., Reading Recovery [Clay 1993]; Right Start [Hiebert et al. 1992]), is built on a strong research foundation. (See Pikulski [1994]; Hiebert and Taylor [2000] for reviews of successful early reading intervention models.) It is important that children who start second grade reading below grade level quickly experience success in reading, and EIR is structured so this happens. The EIR model works on a three-day cycle. Its predictable structure provides consistency for struggling readers, and helps build their confidence. During the three-day cycle of lessons, students are supported through the following practices:

▶ active engagement

▶ systematic word recognition instruction

▶ coaching in word-recognition strategies

- repeated reading for fluency

- comprehension and vocabulary instruction

- one-on-one reading practice

- regular monitoring of progress

Active Engagement

Students are busy participating in reading experiences throughout the 20-minute, small-group session. Within this time period, students engage in four activities that address different elements essential to learning to read. This twenty-minute session is considered to be acceleration, unlike remediation, and implies that the children receiving this intervention can learn to read before they fall way behind. In EIR, children typically enjoy the small-group routine and stay actively engaged during the lesson.

Systematic Word-Recognition Instruction

The teacher begins with an emphasis on letter-by-letter sequential decoding and progresses to an emphasis on decoding by onset and rime. A brief review of the learning-to-read process, in which phonemic awareness and decoding abilities play a large part, was discussed earlier in this chapter.

Some phonemic awareness refinement and phonics instruction is done through word work after students have read their EIR story, but another big emphasis of word-recognition instruction in EIR lessons is on coaching children to use multiple decoding strategies as they attempt to depend on themselves in the reading of actual text. In a national study of accomplished teachers and effective schools, Taylor and colleagues (2000) found that phonics instruction in isolation is important but not sufficient. The best grade 1 and 2 teachers and teachers in the most effective schools were frequently observed coaching children in the use of word-recognition strategies as they got stuck on words while reading.

Coaching the Use of Multiple Word-Recognition Strategies

Coaching is used while children read and involves the teacher modeling, asking questions, or giving prompts related to words children don't know how to decode. This coaching enables children to succeed at figuring out a word they don't instantly recognize while they are reading. Typically, when a teachers asks children, "What do you do when you come to a word you don't know?" they will say, "Sound it out." That is one good strategy, but we want them to realize there are other things readers do when they come to hard words. As coaches, teachers need to learn to prompt children to use a variety of different word-recognition strategies and not overrely a single strategy.

Coaching also helps children learn to self-monitor their word-recognition attempts. For example, if a child comes to a word, reads it incorrectly, and then corrects it, this is a good example of self-monitoring. Complementing children for their attempts (e.g., "Good checking, how did you know to try that word

Elkonin Sound Box Activity

This activity is used to develop phonemic awareness as well as letter name knowledge, letter sound knowledge, and letter-by-letter sequential decoding in writing words. Children listen for sounds in words from the stories they are reading and write the letters for these sounds in a string of boxes. For example, if a story is about a hen, the teacher might ask them to listen for the sounds in *hen* as they say the word and then write *h* in the first box, *e* in the second and *n* in the third. This technique, along with the other word work activities mentioned here, comes after reading the story. They all are described in detail in Chapter 3.

Cunningham's Making Words Technique

After about three months, teachers shift their literacy instruction from Sound Boxes to Making Words (Cunningham 2009). In this activity, the teacher hands out letters printed on paper, cards, or tiles and has the children change one letter at a time as they build different words and end up with a word from the story. In a story about thunder, students might make *net, ten, hen, den, nut, hut, thud,* and finally, *thunder*. This activity helps children learn to pay attention to the sequence of letters within words and helps them grasp the alphabetic principle. At the end of the word-building activity, the children sort these words by first letter, and more importantly, by phonograms.

Guided Writing for Sounds

With this technique, children write a group sentence early on or an individual sentence later in the year about the story with coaching support from the teacher. After reading *Mr. Gumpy's Outing* (1945) by Jon Burningham (1990), one student might write, "At the end they all sit down and have tea," with help from the teacher on the *ow* in *down*, the *ea* in *tea,* and so on. By trying to write for sounds, as they also communicate an idea about the story, children refine their phonemic awareness, develop their understanding of the alphabetic principle, and learn letter sound correspondences.

again?") is an integral part of the instruction, as are the praise and questions that encourage children to be aware of the strategies they are using to make sense of texts. Students need to learn how to notice instances when words they say don't make sense in the context of the story or don't look like the actual word they are trying to read. Part of self-monitoring is learning to cross-check; that is, not only being sure a word looks like the word on the page but also being sure that a word makes sense in the story, or vice versa.

Coaching to Develop Student Independence

An important part of coaching students in word-recognition strategies is to release responsibility to the children as soon as possible. Typically at first, you will have to model, or demonstrate for them, how to use different strategies.

You will have to suggest a particular strategy they might try for a particular word (e.g., *Is there a chunk you recognize?* Or, *Look at the picture.* Or, *What would make sense?*) or perhaps even start to use a strategy for them (e.g., /f/ /ee/ in *feet*). Often, however, teachers inadvertently help struggling readers too much for too long, and the students don't learn to depend on themselves. As the year progresses, we need to use more general prompts (e.g., *What can you do?* Or, *Look at that again.*) and focus on our wait time to be sure we give students enough opportunity to try to problem solve and figure out words for themselves. I know as I am coaching children, I feel successful when they come to a hard word and don't look up at me for the answer. It's important to praise them for this independence and to remind them that this is what they need to continue to do when they are reading on their own.

Repeated Reading for Fluency

Students read and reread texts—a single book over three days. They read stories chorally, by taking turns, with a partner, and independently, helps them experience fluent reading as well as the feeling of success. Children also begin to develop automaticity for some of the higher frequency words they encounter (e.g., *the, is, and*).

Benchmarks to Reach by Midyear and End of Year

You will read more about the transition phase of EIR in Chapter 5 but here is a brief preview: By January, or earlier if students are ready, the EIR routine alternates between repeated reading of a "new" story and transition reading for independence. At this point, teachers work with two children at a time as they read a story for the first time. Teachers need to focus on exerting patience, giving enough wait time, and using general prompts as they support children in their attempts to use strategies to read unfamiliar text. It is important that the children show themselves as soon as possible that they can pick up a book they have never read and actually read it and feel successful doing so. In second grade, we want students to be reading on a solid second-grade level by the end of the school year and to leave at the end of the year with the feeling that they can continue to pick up books over the summer and read them successfully.

One-on-One Reading

Another part of EIR that is essential for children's success is one-on-one coaching throughout the year, as each child rereads their "newest" EIR story aloud, someone is at his side listening, encouraging, and coaching. A coach can be an educational assistant, volunteer, or older student who has received training. With this individualized attention, the child is unable to "hide" behind someone else's voice and builds confidence in his or her ability to read. This helps the student build reading fluency and experience success as a reader.

Training one-on-one coaches is essential. See Chapter 9 for tips on training educational assistants, parents, community volunteers, and older students.

Comprehension Instruction and Vocabulary Development

Teaching beginning struggling readers to read for meaning is very important, but it is sometimes neglected because of the focus on teaching students to "break the code." To send the message that reading for meaning is what reading is all about, teachers in EIR lessons discuss the meanings of potentially unfamiliar words they come across in the story and ask one question about the story every day that either expands students' comprehension of the story, stretches their thinking, relates the story to their lives, or involves them in summarizing. As students answer the questions, the teacher coaches them to elaborate on their ideas. I call this part of the EIR lesson "coaching for comprehension." Since there is a lot to cover in the 20-minute EIR lesson, teachers don't try to give all children a chance to answer every day. However, over the three days spent on a story, teachers are able to give all children a chance to answer one of the questions they ask.

Regular Monitoring of Progress

Regular assessment of student progress is important to a child's success in the EIR program and is a hallmark of effective teachers and schools (Lipson et al. 2004; Pressley et al. 2003; Taylor et al. 2000). Teachers need to frequently monitor students' reading abilities to know when to fine-tune their instruction. They may need to provide more help or they may need to release more responsibility to the students to accelerate their reading growth. The teacher takes an oral reading check about every other story on every student. (See Chapter 7 for more on assessment.) Based on research, children in the basic EIR model who are able to read their EIR story with at least 90 percent accuracy after spending three days on it are making good progress in learning to read (Taylor et al. 1992).

Oral reading checks are difficult to analyze for patterns of errors in grade 2 when the children are in the repeated reading phase of the EIR model. Students often have parts of the story memorized, so a teacher gets an inaccurate picture of the errors they would tend to make if they were reading more independently. By the transition phase, however, teachers can begin to analyze oral reading errors. This is described more in Chapter 5.

How the EIR Model Fits Within a Balanced Literacy Block

Let's take a look at how you might fit EIR lessons into your day by organizing your instruction around 110- to 120-minute reading blocks.

Reading Block: A Sample Schedule

May Holder has a 100-minute reading block in the morning. She spends from about 30 minutes a day on a whole-group lesson that includes high levels of student response. She spends about 70 minutes a day on four guided reading groups before lunch and 20 minutes on one EIR group after lunch (which is a second shot of quality instruction for her struggling readers). Here is an example of her schedule.

Reading Block
Mary Holder's Sample Schedule

9:00–9:30   Whole-Group Lesson

▶ Using a selection from basal reader, target a comprehension strategy, teach vocabulary at point of contact in the selection, discuss answers to high-level questions, and review learning activities for independent work time.

9:30–9:50   Small-Group 1

▶ Using a story in a text at students' reading level, provide phonics instruction as needed, coach students in word-recognition strategies as they read their leveled text, discuss vocabulary at point of contact in the story, provide follow-up instruction to the comprehension strategy targeted in a whole-group lesson, and discuss answers to high-level questions on leveled text.

9:50–10:05   Small-Group 2

▶ Follow same strategies as for small group 1.

10:05–10:25   Small-Group 3

▶ Follow same strategies as for small group 1.

10:25–10:40   Small-Group 4

▶ Follow same strategies as for small group 1.

12:00–12:20   EIR Lesson

▶ Follow EIR strategies. (Note that these students were also in one of the small groups.)

In the next chapter, you'll see how May, Leah, and Diane make the content and pedagogy of effective reading instruction—and the principles of EIR—come alive in their whole-group and small-group lessons. In Chapters 3, 5 and 6, we look at excellent reading instruction again so you can see it through the lens of the intervention lessons. In Chapter 8 we also return to our three teachers' classrooms to see how they organize their day to be able to provide EIR lessons to their students who need more reading support and to offer motivating independent literacy learning activities to all of their students.

DISCUSS WITH YOUR COLLEAGUES

1. Discuss the Stages of Word Recognition in Figure 1-1 that is described in the section of this chapter that reviews the learning-to-read process.

2. Share with colleagues your current understandings about teaching reading. What was striking in this chapter? What changed your thinking?

3. When you consider implementing EIR, what are the challenges? What support systems are already in place in your school to lean on (parent volunteer programs, PTO, collaboration with fifth-grade teachers whose students might coach, etc.)?

Meet the Teachers

· ·

The Differentiated Lessons and Teacher Collaboration That Support EIR

In this chapter, I highlight three teachers—May Holder, Leah Davis, and Diane Swanson—who are connected to my Early Intervention in Reading (EIR) framework and to my work on effective instruction and school change in reading (Taylor 2010c). I share their words about the benefits of engaging in professional development with colleagues, because intervening with your struggling second-grade readers can be easier if you share successes, questions, and concerns with other teachers about reading instruction. Intervention models are often not effective because they are insufficiently embedded in a school-wide vision of sound reading instruction. These three teachers teach in different

schools with different student populations who have different needs. The following teachers' vignettes paint a backdrop for the EIR lessons and show how effective classroom reading instruction for all students supports and echoes the reading content and pedagogy of the EIR lessons.

Diversity in the Highlighted Teachers' Schools

Teacher	Years Teaching	School Setting	Percent of Students Who Receive Subsidized Lunch	Percent English Language Learners
May	25	Suburban	47	16
Leah	12	Urban	80	46
Diane	5	Rural	63	12

Table 2-1 Diversity in the Highlighted Teachers' Schools

The Teachers

May Holder teaches second grade at suburban Woodlawn Elementary School where 47 percent of the students receive subsidized lunch and 16 percent speak English as a second language. May has been teaching for twenty-five years, worked in study groups as part of a schoolwide reading improvement project for three years, and learned how to deliver EIR intervention instruction through participation in an EIR study group in the second year of her school's change process. In the third year of the school change project, May's students grew by an average of nine normal curve equivalents (NCEs) on the Gates MacGinitie Reading test from fall to spring, ending the school year with a mean comprehension score at the 55th NCE, or 60th percentile.

Leah Davis teaches second grade at Lincoln Elementary, an urban school where 80 percent of the students receive subsidized lunch and 46 percent are English language learners (ELLs), primarily Hmong, Somali, and Spanish speakers. Leah has been teaching for twelve years, and was new to Lincoln in the second year of the school reform in reading project. She learned how to teach EIR intervention lessons in her first year at Lincoln. Her students grew by a mean of seven NCEs during their second grade year, ending the year with a mean NCE comprehension score of 50 (50th percentile, up from the 43rd NCE, or 37th percentile, in the fall).

Diane Swanson teaches second grade at Wheeler Elementary, a school in a small rural town where 63 percent of the students receive subsidized lunch and 12 percent are ELLs, primarily native Spanish speakers. Linda has been teaching for five years, and she learned how to teach EIR intervention lessons in the second year of her school's reading improvement project. Diane's students grew by a mean of nine NCEs during the third year of the school-based reform effort, ending the year with a mean NCE comprehension score of 55 (which corresponds to the 60th percentile).

Common Factors in Students' Reading Gains

These teachers have different routines and work in different settings, but you'll notice there are commonalities that are instrumental to the success of their teaching and the reading achievements of their students. For example, these teachers are:

▶ Teaching reading with a focus on meaning

▶ Providing sufficient modeling, coaching, and guided practice

▶ Giving students many opportunities to respond and participate

▶ Differentiating instruction

▶ Using the EIR model with students who come in the fall at risk

▶ Providing students with independent work that is appropriate for their level as readers, engaging, and designed to deepen their understanding. That is, not busywork!

▶ Involving parents and caregivers in a daily minimum of 20 minutes of reading at home

▶ Collaborating with other teachers in teaching and in professional learning

Teacher Talk

The Influence of Collaborative Professional Learning on Teaching Practice

Whether you choose to launch into the early intervention lessons on your own or with colleagues, the following are some encouraging comments from other teachers who have engaged in professional development with peers, including EIR reflection sessions, to help them improve their overall reading instruction.

> **MAY:** I do a lot more strategy instruction than I used to, a lot more modeling, and I have a better idea of how to release responsibility to my students as they work toward independence. I am more purposeful in my instruction and my students, in turn, understand the purpose for what they are learning. Also, I have more flexible grouping and differentiated instruction than in the past. Now, students aren't reading the same book or doing the same thing all the time. It varies, depending on their needs.
>
> I have been more in depth with my questioning and I am asking and getting students to ask many higher-level questions. My book clubs have paid off because students are having awesome discussions on their own. Last year I made up the questions for most of the year, but this year students were ready sooner to come up with their own.
>
> My vocabulary instruction has changed; I teach it in context to make it more real world and meaningful for my students. My word-recognition instruction has changed; I use Word Boxes and Making Words that I learned in EIR with all of my students who need phonics instruction.
>
> The kids are expected to read at home for 20 minutes a day and the parents sign a sheet [verifying] that this is happening. When the kids discuss

what they are reading, many parents are amazed at the growth and progress their kids are making.

I have especially seen growth with the lower students who have been in EIR and who weren't confident in the beginning of the year. Higher expectations for myself and my students have promoted student achievement. It is fun to see that they can do more than I might have expected.

LEAH: I work hard to make the classroom environment nurturing and to encourage the love of reading in all of my students. I do a lot with literature, even in the content areas, and we also go on the Internet together. My students are developing the joy of reading. I like to see their faces light up. I also try to link school to student's lives by constantly making connections between home, school, and the community.

Talking with others is helpful; it expands on what you know and you get to see other ways of instructing. The more we communicate as a staff, the better. This professional learning has helped me really understand how to watch a child and see what happens.

I partner with my parents in every way. I always invite parents to come into the classroom and see what their child is doing. I call them as well. This is our little community, and I feel that it is very important to keep everyone connected.

The more positive words you give children, the more they want to achieve. Their reading scores have really gone up, students feel that they are achieving, and this is building up their confidence. Also the children have more enthusiasm for reading.

DIANE: Planning has been critical; if I don't plan and read the stories ahead of time, it doesn't go well; student engagement is also a critical element of my reading instruction, so I have my students reading or responding to texts during most of the regular reading block; having guided reading at students' level; giving students many opportunities to read texts for enjoyment as well as for practicing fluency.

It has been challenging to let go of a lot of things that are in the basal. It feels sort of like losing a safety net. But by letting go of some things, there is time for more valuable things

I now take running records regularly as students read in guided reading groups. I do more with summarizing, reciprocal teaching, and Question-Answer Relationships (QARs). I ask more high-level questions. The kids are doing more writing in response to their reading than they have in the past.

I have expanded my book clubs. I have two reading groups [that] are doing their own thing. I sit back and help only when I need to. The kids are coming up with their own questions and leading their own discussions.

The main challenge we continually have is meeting individual needs, and my twenty-two students are performing at different spots. There's always a huge gap between your high and your low, which makes it difficult. I now teach EIR lessons and I wouldn't give that up. I think the EIR model has been so beneficial for the low readers because they have begun to see themselves as fluent readers and are feeling successful.

Some of the best experts teach right next to you. In second grade, we share ideas on just about everything related to improving our reading instruction. We also share information on the best way to reach specific kids. A common language, a shared vision, a focus on high-level questioning and challenging books have been the most valuable for the school as a whole.

I make a personal call to parents at least quarterly with a positive comment about each student. I send home weekly progress reports and information about reading and math. The grade 2 team sends home a book bag so kids can read at home. I attached a higher-level question bookmark to the book bag at the beginning of the year, so the parents know what kinds of questions to ask their kids. During the summer, we have a book checkout in the library.

Their level of independence is awesome and the way they use strategies and analyze and interact with what they read is beyond my expectations. I have seen big changes in the reading journals they write in every day after independent reading. At the beginning of the year the students didn't explain their ideas very well, and they now give many insights and wonderful explanations. Also, I see kids more willing to take risks at answering questions, to express their opinions, and to challenge others on answers. They are questioning what things mean because of the clarifying we do all of the time. They are transferring this over to science class and my read-aloud time as well.

I want to emphasize that the beauty of EIR is that it can reside in many different kinds of classrooms, complementing a reading workshop approach or any other balanced literacy model. As you read these lesson overviews, remember they don't capture every teaching move but are here to show you how different teachers incorporate elements of effective reading instruction into their teaching based on their own styles and, or course, their students' needs. Notice how the teachers integrate the various components of content, including instruction in vocabulary and comprehension strategies, as well as elements of pedagogy including direct teaching and coaching; differentiation; and intellectually challenging independent, partner, and small-group activities.

Comprehension Strategies Instruction: Reciprocal Teaching

The goal of our instruction is for students to take on the responsibility of learning to read. If we try to move students too quickly from demonstration to independent practice, however, it often doesn't work. To scaffold students, May relies on the reciprocal teaching strategies (Palincsar and Brown 1986) and sets a goal of February for her students to be using them independently. She introduces the four primary strategies of clarifying, predicting, generating questions, and summarizing one at a time from October through January.

Clarifying

In October, May introduces her second graders to the strategy of clarifying understandings in a whole-class lesson: "When we read, we come across words or ideas that we don't understand very well. As good readers, we need to clarify these things that are confusing." She models by talking aloud about a confusing idea from the basal story that they are reading as a whole group: "Today, when we meet in small groups, we'll practice clarifying some more."

Small-Group Lessons

Going forward, May connects the whole-group and small-group work by having students practice clarifying with a story. She gives students sticky notes and has them write down words or ideas that are confusing that they then share at the end of the small-group lesson. After a few weeks, her second graders are gaining confidence with the strategy.

Partner Work

Later in October, May has students take on more responsibility for using the strategy. She pairs students up and tells them, "Keep reading the story we were reading together. If your partner asks what something means, you should try to answer your partner's question. Your partner's words will help you clarify your understanding."

Predicting

In November, May focuses on the second reciprocal teaching strategy: predicting. With the whole group, she teaches about making predictions as a way to get students curious about a text. At a small-group lesson, she reviews making predictions by asking, "Why do we make predictions?" Students answer, "To see if we are thinking the right way. So we understand better." May asks, "Are we always right in our predictions?" A student answers, "No, but then we read to find out what happens." May reminds students about one of the purposes of making predictions, "You get more excited about what you are reading when you make predictions because this helps you be actively involved in your reading."

May asks students to predict and share with their partners what they think might happen next. A few students take turns sharing aloud. May provides feedback, "You are doing an excellent job and I can tell you are anxious to read more." She then tells students to go back to their desks, finish reading the book they are reading in their small group, and write answers to the higher-level questions on the board that she has written for their group.

Generating Questions

In December, May focuses on generating in-the-book and in-your-head questions (Raphael, Highfield, and Au 2006) with the whole class. She also teaches students to distinguish between low-level (literal) and high-level questions. She asks a small group, "What kind of questions are these that you have written down?" Students say, "In-the-book." She replies, "Yes, these are 'in-the-book' questions because we can go back into the book and find the answers. What are 'in-the-head' questions? Yes, these are questions where you have to use the ideas in your head to help you answer them."

She returns to the purpose of generating questions during or after reading. "Why does it help to write down questions when we read?" A student answers, "They help me remember what I read and help me understand it better." At their seats during independent work time, students are to write some literal-level and high-level questions about their small-group story. They label them as in-the-book or in-the-head questions and pick one high-level question to ask and discuss in their small group the next day.

Summarizing Narrative Text

In January, May focuses on summarizing. For narrative text, she talks about summarizing the beginning with characters and setting, the middle with problems and events, and the end with the resolution of the problem and author's message (if there is one). She talks about not giving too many details but just the important things: "Write the beginning here with me and then start the middle when you get back to your seats."

Summarizing Informational Text

In January, students are reading a *National Geographic Kids* magazine in a large-group lesson, and May focuses on summarizing informational text. She talks about summarizing the main ideas and important supporting details and says, "I can tell you are excited to learn about lizards. Today we are going to think about what the author wants us to learn or know." May reads the first section and asks students to follow with their eyes as she reads. "Our strategy is to find the main idea of this section. What do you think the author wants us to know?" A student responds, "He wants us to learn about lizards." May asks the student to elaborate, "That is the topic, but give me a more specific, important idea about lizards." Students take turns responding. May clarifies, "The author wants us to learn that lizards adapt to survive. We will read about the first lizard together. What is the horned lizard's adaptation?" Students respond and May coaches. "The horned lizard has adapted to look like a frog. It also blends in with rocks."

She gives students in groups of three different sections of the magazine to read and summarize. Students move around the room to find a place to work collaboratively. May explains to them, "Decide on jobs and get to work." She differentiates instruction by working with a group of six students in the front of the room who need more support reading the magazine and summarizing their section. Periodically, she checks in with the other groups.

After 15 minutes, she calls students to the back of the room. "Okay, let's hear the thoughts in your heads." She then asks one group, "Which lizard did you have? Tell us about a blue-tailed skink. What is its adaptation?" One student from the group reads what they have written. She moves on to other groups with other lizards. At the end she says, "Do you think the author did a good job helping us learn about adaptations for lizards?" Students respond with thumbs up or down (active responding). Most thumbs are up.

"Now I want you to respond to this article in journals at your desks. Tell me two new things that you learned that were interesting or surprising to you. Use your own words," May prompts. Students move to their desks. May differentiates instruction by working with a few students who need more support to succeed at this task. She says to one student, "As you are writing make sure you name that lizard in your sentence so we know which lizard you are talking about." She also walks around the room giving feedback to students. She reads a student's response and demonstrates enthusiasm by saying, "Cool. That was surprising to me, too." She then tells students, "Sit with a partner and tell each other two things that you learned or that surprised you."

Ready for Reciprocal Teaching

In February, May reviews the four reciprocal teaching reading strategies she has previously taught students as they talk about the nonfiction and fiction books they are reading. She now focuses on helping them use all of these strategies as they read. They have an open-ended reciprocal teaching response sheet they write on in whole-group and small-group lessons that has room for them to clarify, predict, generate questions, and summarize.

May works from a clear plan for teaching her students reciprocal teaching strategies. She introduces one strategy a month from October through January before she has students use all of the reciprocal teaching strategies at one time. As you reflect on May's strategy teaching, think about how her EIR lessons fit within this reading instruction. That is, the children in her intervention lessons are reaping the benefits of all this other strategy work.

Encouraging High-Level Talk: Book Clubs

May gets students involved in high-level talk and writing about texts through book clubs that they engage in during independent work time. She uses cards with prompts printed on them to teach students how to agree and politely disagree as well as how to add to someone's idea. She also teaches them about not talking too much, being a good listener, and making sure that everyone gets a chance to talk. She teaches students how to take turns being the discussion leader and how to bring "juicy" questions to their book club meetings. She differentiates instruction by starting book clubs with her above-average readers group in the fall, average readers in the winter, and lowest-ability readers in the spring. She has students who have already learned how to take part in book clubs coach students who are just learning.

In November, May coaches her above-average readers as they are learning how to work in book clubs. One group is discussing the book, *Stone Fox* (Gardiner 1980). As students talk about questions that May has written for them, she coaches with phrases such as, "Does anyone have anything else to add? How is that a connection? Explain some more."

May also helps student learn how to come up with their own "juicy" questions for book clubs. For the book, *Stone Fox*, a student offers the question, "Who came to the house?" May asks, "What type of question is this?" A student says, "Lower-level question." May asks, "How can we change it into a higher-level question?" May coaches, "If it starts with 'why' it is often higher level. Think about how we could change it." A student comes up with, "Why did the man come to their house?"

May ends the lesson by assigning the book club chapters to read for their book club meeting the day after next. She asks them to write good discussion questions on index cards and bring them to their next meeting as well. After a few months, these students are able to meet on their own and May checks in on their conversations a few times as they meet.

May takes time to explicitly teach her students how to engage in book club discussions. Also, at first, she makes up the book club questions for her students. It takes a few months before her above-average readers are coming up with their own questions and taking part in student-led book club discussions on their own.

Developing Vocabulary: Using Context Clues

Students are sitting on the floor in a large group. May says, "We are going to talk about context clues today. Context clues are ways to figure out words we are not sure about. Clues, or signal words, around a word help you figure out what words mean." May points to the chart "Using Context Clues," which is hanging in her room. She tells the class, "I will model all this information for you so you can do it without my assistance." She models by talking aloud as she tries to figure out the word *scowled*. "I will look back at that sentence again. I think *scowled* means that he looks at her in an angry way. I used the clues around that word, like 'did not look happy,' to help me figure that out. Doing this will help you understand what is going on in the text. We will reread the page and use context clues to help us identify what *sift* means." They also talk about the word *butcher* and the clues they used to figure out the word's meaning.

May concludes by saying, "When you are reading during language arts, social studies, or math, all of these areas have words that we don't know the meaning of so think about using context clues. Make your best inference or use your best thinking to figure out what a word is. But if that doesn't work and the word seems really important, you can look it up in the dictionary or glossary" (which is a transition to reading in the content areas).

In small-group lessons, May continues to talk about using context clues to figure out words. She writes *stroke* on the whiteboard and passes out sticky notes to each student. She tells them, "When you come across that word in your reading during independent work time, write a page number down. Use context clues to help you figure out that word. There are at least two words in the story that second graders do not know. Find out what *stroke* means and find one more word as you read. There is a glossary in the back of the book if the context clues don't help you."

May does an excellent job of talking aloud as she models and talks about transfer of reading strategies they practice to reading on their own or in another subject area.

Activating Background Knowledge and Making Connections

Leah Davis has a 110-minute reading block. She begins with a whole-group lesson that lasts 30 to 45 minutes. She then spends 15 to 20 minutes with each of three guided reading groups and 20 minutes on one EIR group, which is a second shot of quality instruction for her struggling readers. The three lessons that follow are taught by Leah; there are two comprehension strategy lessons and one explicit phonics lesson.

Comprehension Strategies Instruction: Activating Background Knowledge and Making Connections

Whole-Group Lesson

Leah says, "Today we'll be talking about a strategy that will help you understand what you are reading. We've been talking about background knowledge, that it is all of our experiences, memories, and knowledge that we bring to our reading. We'll be talking about a way to use background knowledge and it's called *making text-to-self connections*. You make connections between something you've read (the text) and something from your personal life. Let's look at a book. With this strategy, you relate something from your life to what you are reading and this helps you understand the story better (purpose). You can use this strategy any time you are reading (transfer). I'm going to read to you and model how I do this because it helps me understand the characters better and what they are doing and why."

Leah reads *The Relatives Came* by Cynthia Rylant (1985) to the class and stops to model as she reads, "This is just like we did when I was a little girl." She shares an experience from her childhood. "This makes me think of when my uncles and aunts would come and visit us and how we would wait for them. So this makes me think they must be very happy just like we were."

Leah continues reading and modeling how she relates the text to her background knowledge. "I can tell that a lot of people are making connections to this story. Remember what connection you made with the book and find a partner and tell them about it." Children share with their partner and then with the group. One student says, "Every time my relatives visit me there are so many hugs I can't get to the kitchen."

Leah explains, "When you read your just-right books during independent work time, I want you to use a sticky note to mark a place where you make a connection." Leah passes out the books for students at their reading level. She meets with two small groups during this time, reading and following up on the comprehension strategy being taught.

Small-Group Lesson

Leah is with a group of six children at the reading table. They are reading a story about a child who is waiting at the airport for her grandmother to arrive on a visit. Children take turns reading and the others are reminded by their teacher to follow along in their books. She watches them to be sure they are in fact reading. Leah says, "Before we go to the next page, you put a sticky note on the page if you make a connection."

Leah coaches students to use word-recognition strategies as they read. When they are not sure of the word *celebrations*, one boy gets it by chunking. When they come to a word no one knows, Leah says, "Let's look closely at this." One boy gets *summer* when he sounds out the letters in the word.

Children continue reading and then share their connections. One student says, "My connections is the smile of the Grandma." Leah coaches by asking the student to elaborate, "Why?" The student adds, "Because it makes me think of my Papa smiling." Another student says, "I can't wait until my Grandma comes from Chicago." Leah offers feedback, "You are doing a good job reading this book and making connections."

Leah does an excellent job of modeling before she gives students the opportunity to actively participate in sharing connections with a partner. She follows up on the strategy covered in a whole group by returning to it in guided reading groups and with independent work activities.

Guided Reading Lesson on Comprehension Monitoring

On a different day, Leah teaches her students about comprehension monitoring. In a small group she says, "We have been working on many comprehension strategies this year. The one we are going to work on today is comprehension monitoring." Leah puts a chart on the table. Students read the questions in unison, "What is it? Why do we do it? When do we use it? How does it help us?" Leah says, "When you are reading and something is confusing, you stop when you don't understand something and fix it." She gives the answer to each of the questions as she talks aloud about comprehension monitoring. She passes out a sheet on the table called "Reasons for Confusion," and explains what she wants students to do. She tells the students they can refer to these questions as they read if they get stuck. She also passes out a vocabulary list for the story and asks students to pay attention to these words as they are reading (vocabulary at point of contact). Students will discuss the words once they have finished reading.

Students read their story, *The Salamander Room* (Mazer 1991), at their own pace. Leah listens to one student read at a time and asks about comprehension monitoring as she listens, "Now was there anything confusing to you as you read that page? I'm not sure that you're quite getting that word." She has the student reread. "That's an /oo/ sound" (she coaches for word recognition). The student figures it out. Leah asks, "So what does *roost* mean?" The student says, "Like lay down and rest." "Yep! Good job. Now does the page make more sense?"

Leah's chart is a good visual tool that students can use to help them remember the what, why, when, and how of a comprehension strategy when they are reading independently. As she listens to students read one-on-one, she coaches them on comprehension monitoring through the questions she asks.

Phonics Lesson

Leah uses Making Words (Cunningham 2009) to teach a phonics lesson to an average-ability group of readers. After passing out the letters students will use to make words, she says *tray*. She asks students to give the sounds of the word. Students say /tr/ and then /ay/. Leah says to add an *s* to the beginning of the word. "Let's sound that word out." She says that they are using consonant blends. They have made the word *stray*. She has them say the blend and then the vowel sounds. She then says the word *strain* and tells them that they are going to leave out a sound and will add a sound. She asks which sound they are leaving out and which sound they are adding. She asks what sound *ai* makes. Leah says the word *train* and asks which sound was left out of *strain* to make the new word. Once the students answer and understand, she moves to the word *trap*.

Students continue to make words. They are to make the word *troll* out of *trap*. A student says that they are to take away the *a* and *p* and add *oll*. Leah praises them for their thinking and then says they are going to start over and make the word *cram*. Then they make the word *cream*. They add a letter to make the word *scream*. She tells them to take away the *am* and make the word *screw*, then *new*. They reread all of the words they made and sort them by consonant blends and by vowel teams. She talks about how knowing these phonics elements will help them decode more words and praises them for their good work.

Diane has a 120-minute reading block. She describes her grouping practices: "I meet with the whole class for 30 to 40 minutes a day. I have four groups that I meet with for about 20 minutes on a daily basis plus two EIR groups. The children in the EIR groups meet with the Title 1 teacher for their regular guided group since I am doing the EIR piece. I have three students who meet with an aide in addition to their guided reading group for word work. I have one student who joins another second-grade class for a high guided reading group and is challenged there. I have two students who go to the learning center to work with the special education teacher for much of their reading time, but I also see those students in one of my guided reading or EIR groups."

Two of Diane's lessons are provided here and focus on summarizing stories and summarizing informational text.

Comprehension: Summarizing Narrative Text

Whole-Group Lesson

Diane reviews the story they read the day before, *The Great Ball Game.* "What is something we could do to help us remember that story?" Students say they could come up with a summary. Diane asks for another instance when they could use a summary (purpose). Students answer, "In the library, at home, telling a friend." Diane asks, "Do you always have to write it down?" Students say, "*No.*" Diane elaborates, "Sometimes you could think about it in your head."

She then helps the students summarize through her coaching prompts. "What is the most important thing you could think about from the beginning? Turn to your partner and tell them who was in the story, where it took place, and what the problem was." Students share with partners. Diane asks, "What did you and your partner talk about? Who were the characters?" Students mention the animals, birds, and bat. Diane asks about the setting and the problem, "Where or when did the story take place? What was the problem?" Students answer and Diane asks, "Who can put all that information into a good sentence?" A student gives a complete sentence, and Diane restates, "Good job. Long ago, the birds and the animals were having an argument about who was the best. Now think about the middle and the ending of the story. What happened and how did they solve the problem?" Students say the animals won because they had the bat. Diane concludes by restating the purpose of summarizing, "By summarizing, I get the story in my head. I won't forget the important parts. What do we also need to tell?" Students say, "The author's message." Diane says, "Tell your partner what message you got from the author." She asks a few students to share what they talked about. One student says, "The littlest person can still be a big help." Another says, "If you are little you can still do big things." Diane says, "Your message may not always be the same because we all have different experiences and this is okay. Good job."

Follow-Up During Independent Work Time

For follow-up work on this study, Diane gives the students questions to answer in their response journals. They are to choose one high-level question to respond to. The questions the students can choose are: *What would you like to say to the birds and animals, and what advice could you give them?* Or, *What problem did the birds and animals have, and what lesson did they learn?* Students write the question they want to answer in their reading response journals. Diane adds, "It will be fun hearing your ideas on these questions." She calls up a small guided reading group as other students begin to write at their seats.

Diane does an excellent job of coaching students on the challenging task of summarizing a story and of restating the purpose of summarizing at the end of the lesson. She reminds them that the author's message is an important part of the summary that often gets left out. The independent work activity gives students the opportunity to engage in high-level thinking and writing about the story they just read.

Comprehension: Summarizing Informational Text

Diane and a few of her students work on summarizing informational text. Diane begins, "Our book is called, *Peanuts*. We are going to learn about peanuts. We are going to read the first section and then summarize that page. Why would we want to summarize that page?" Students answer, "So we learn. It will help you remember it. When you are reading at home or in the library you can use it." Diane adds, "When you are in third grade and you study for a test you could use this strategy."

Diane teaches students two important words to establish the topic of a page and then has them generate a sentence or two around these two words that summarizes the important ideas on the page. Having students go from topic to main idea statement is a good way for them to learn how to summarize informational text (Taylor 1986).

Students begin reading. Diane reminds them, "As you read, think of a couple of important words and about how you will write a sentence or two that summarizes this page." She coaches in word recognition as a student gets stuck on a word. "Remember the *e-a*, What does *e-a* say?" The student decodes the word correctly.

After students have read the first section, Diane asks, "Who can give one or two words that this page is all about?" A student answers, "Dirt and water." Diane coaches, "Was this page about mostly about dirt and water? What was this page about?" Another student says, "Peanuts and seeds." Diane prompts, "What sentence could we make using these two words?" A student gives a sentence, "Peanuts are seeds." Diane asks, "Is that what this page is telling us?" Students agree that it is. Diane continues by adding a second important idea, "We could also tell where they grow. They grow underground. This helps us remember what this page was about."

Students continue to read the next sections of the text and they stop to summarize as they go. Diane coaches as they work through the book. She asks students to come up with two important words that the section is mostly about and then asks them to turn these into one or two sentences that summarize the section as they did with her. She also models comprehension monitoring. She states, "I'm confused. I'm not sure what that word means (*sow*). I have to make it make sense or I can't go on. Let's reread. *In the spring I get my garden ready by planting my seeds. Sow* must mean to plant the seeds."

Independent Follow-up Activity

Diane tells students that during independent work time with the educational assistant, they are going to choose their own animal books at their reading levels (differentiated instruction). "Find a just-right book on an animal you like on the back table. Read a page or section of the book that interests you and use the open-ended response sheet to write a summary of that page just like we did in whole group. Give the topic and then turn the topic into a sentence. Also, find answers to these two questions: *What does your animal eat? Where does your animal live?* Finally, write down one interesting fact you learned about your animal. The educational assistant can help you look on the Internet for more information on your animal as well."

@ @ @

In Chapter 8, we return to May, Leah, and Diane's classrooms. We learn about their daily reading schedules that include the EIR lessons they provide to their students who need more support. We also learn about the motivating, independent learning activities they set up for their students to engage in as they work with guided reading and EIR groups.

Making a Schoolwide Commitment to Second-Grade Readers

Before we jump into the EIR lesson how-tos, let's take a moment to think about your own school, and how you might collaborate with one or more of your colleagues on this venture.

The best teaching possible comes from schools in which teachers develop a shared set of understandings and beliefs about teaching and learning in general, and teaching reading in particular. Considerable research in the last decade has identified the following characteristics of schoolwide reading programs that support teachers' abilities to increase students' reading abilities. These schools have

▶ A unified vision for teaching reading in every grade and a cohesive, schoolwide program (Consortium for Responsible School Change 2005; Taylor et al. 2005)

▶ A substantial number of minutes and designated blocks of time devoted to reading instruction across different grades during the school day (Taylor et al. 2000)

▶ A schoolwide assessment plan in which student data is collected and used regularly to inform instruction (Pressley et al. 2003; Taylor et al. 2000; Taylor et al. 2002)

▶ Interventions in place to meet the needs of students who are experiencing reading difficulties, who have special education needs, and who are ELLs (Foorman and Torgesen 2001; Mathes et al. 2005; Taylor et al. 2000)

▶ Effective parent partnerships (Edwards 2004; Taylor et al. 2002)

It is ideal to have an effective schoolwide vision of reading in place, whereby common goals, time to work together, and a culture of peer support are part of your school's DNA. And yet, an individual teacher working hard on her own to enhance her practice can make a huge difference in the lives of students in her class.

Nevertheless, keep in mind that as May, Leah, Diane, and so many other teachers will attest, working with colleagues can provide amazing support. It's hard to examine and critique your own practice. Trusted colleagues can watch you teach, give you feedback, point out your strengths, and offer ideas to enhance your instruction in certain areas. This support helps you look closely at your practice, make modifications, and in the end, teach as effectively as possible so all of your students become skilled, motivated readers.

In Chapter 9 I provide more details on how to set up monthly sessions with colleagues, teach educational assistants or volunteers how to serve as one-on-one coaches, and enlist the support of parents in their children's learning-to-read efforts. Consider exploring the content, pedagogy, and interpersonal skills of exemplary teachers further. Professional books and research articles abound on many of the components of effective reading instruction discussed in this chapter and in Chapter 1. For ongoing professional learning or study groups, see the Recommended Professional Readings provided in the reference section at the back of this book.

DISCUSS WITH YOUR COLLEAGUES

1. Discuss each of the three teachers described in this chapter. What do you like about their lessons? What questions do you have? Discuss questions raised.

2. Is there one strand you'd like to focus on changing in your own teaching? For example, connecting whole-class, small-group, and independent work? Or improving the quality of book discussion in your class?

The Three-Day Lesson Routine

• •

Now that we have looked at effective reading instruction for all students in May, Leah, and Diane's classrooms, let's look at the daily routines of EIR lessons that they also teach, the rationale behind them, and some information to get you started. I'm putting a lot of my advice in bulleted lists because I encourage you to dip in and out of this book for reference as you launch EIR. First, let's recap four foundational ideas:

▶ With EIR, you accelerate students' reading progress based on the same effective reading instruction you use with all students—this is not about remediation. Students who come to second grade not yet reading independently at a first-grade level will need the basic EIR procedures described in this chapter and in Chapter 5 in order to be reading at a second-grade level by the end of the school year. Students who come to second grade reading independently but who need more support to be reading solidly at grade level by the end of the year will need the accelerated EIR procedures described in Chapter 6.

▶ Students who are struggling with reading get an extra shot of quality, small-group reading instruction. These children are getting this support in addition to (not instead of) other whole-group, small-group, and one-on-one attention.

▶ Engaging children's books are chosen for the lessons (see the sample book lists in Chapter 4 and in the DVD teacher resources to guide you).

▶ Children who come to second grade not yet able to read independently get the help they need. Without solid intervention lessons, these children are likely to not be reading on a second-grade level by the end of second grade.

Getting Started: FAQs

In Chapter 7, you will find more information on determining which children might benefit from EIR. For now, here are some questions teachers commonly ask about setting up the groups.

How many students are in a group?

Each group can have from five to seven students, seven being the maximum. If there are more than seven children in your room who need EIR lessons, I would recommend finding a way to have two groups instead of just one. If you have Title 1 at your school, perhaps the Title 1 teacher can take one group and you can take the other. Then you can periodically switch groups so you have a sense of the strengths and weaknesses of all your readers who need additional support to become successful readers.

What if I have a bunch of second graders who need EIR?

With two EIR groups, teachers find it works well to put the faster-progressing students in one group and the slower-progressing students in the other. This grouping allows for all learners to learn at about the same pace; the faster-moving students won't call out answers at the expense of the slower-moving students. Also, the slower-moving students are less inclined to feel discouraged if they do not experience others in their group catching on more quickly.

The students in the faster-moving group may include a student who will be taken out of EIR before the end of the school year because they have benefitted from EIR lessons. Guidelines to help you decide if a child no longer needs EIR lessons are provided in Chapter 5.

Who should teach the EIR students?

As hard as it is to teach two EIR groups, should you find you need to do this, I cannot recommend that one of the groups be taught by an instructional aide. Children at risk of reading failure desperately need quality, supplemental reading instruction, which is in addition to instruction from the regular reading program, and which is provided by certified teachers.

What advice do you have in regard to English Language Learners and EIR?

Often the question comes up as how to handle English language learners (ELLs) and fall placement in EIR. Even if ELLs do relatively poorly on the fall assessment, I would put them in an EIR group in the fall unless they have the opportunity to learn to read in their first language. You do not want to take the chance of preventing any student from learning to read by postponing their participation in EIR to a later time, such as after the first of the year. Also, I have found that ELLs generally do well in EIR (Taylor 2001).

How do students in special education fare with EIR?

I have also found that EIR works well with students with a learning disability. No modifications to the program are recommended.

However, students who are developmentally and cognitively delayed learn well in EIR, but more predictable texts are typically needed than those used in regular EIR lessons to keep the children feeling successful. I would start out with the regular books at EIR Level A and switch to more predictable books, if needed, as the regular EIR stories at Levels B and C get longer and harder. EIR book levels are discussed in Chapter 4 and summarized in Table 4-2.

Do the children in EIR groups feel stigmatized?

Over the many years I've been implementing and researching EIR, teachers report that the children do not feel stigmatized. In fact, children love the fast pace, interesting stories, and feelings of success that they experience in EIR lessons. Children who no longer need EIR lessons because they are reading on grade level often do not want to give the group up. All children are in small groups with their teacher, so no one seems to think much about who is with the teacher when. But the children in EIR lessons like the extra time with their teacher if she is the one teaching the EIR group.

What's the optimum time of the year to start EIR?

It is best to begin EIR in October. However, if you have just bought or been given this book and it is February, then for you, February would be the best time to begin. (It's just not a good idea to start any later in the year than March.) For a February start, you would begin with books at EIR Level C. If these books are too challenging because you have not had students in EIR in the fall, you may have to drop back to Level B books. However, one of the major problems I have seen in the hundreds of second-grade classrooms I have visited over the past 20 years is that teachers often have their students, and especially their struggling readers, reading books that are too easy for them. Remember, in the EIR model we want to challenge students and get them to "glue to the print" so they can figure out how to sound out words as quickly as possible so they can gain meaning from text.

What do I do with second graders who are on the borderline of needing intervention?

There are also accelerated EIR strategies for students who can read independently on an end-of-first-grade reading level when they enter second grade but may still be struggling with word-recognition accuracy or fluency, who have difficulty comprehending what they read, and who would benefit from additional reading support. For these students, you would use the basic three-day routine described, starting with Level D books instead of Level A books, and the routine for transition to independent reading starting with Level F books. The second-grade accelerated EIR strategies are described in Chapter 6.

What's the best way for me to begin to build my confidence with EIR?

After you reread through the three-day set of procedures for the basic second grade teaching routines in Figure 3-1, read the detailed Day 1 procedures that follow and watch the corresponding Day 1 video clips on the accompanying DVD. Soon, the EIR routines will seem very natural, and, as many teachers have reported, you will feel that the extra work on your part is worth the effort! For the past 20 years, I have consistently found that teachers, by February, are very excited about the progress they see their struggling readers making.

How do I know when I am ready to actually teach the lessons?

Once you have read this book, you may not feel completely ready to conduct the lessons, but I have found the best way to learn about EIR procedures is to just jump in and try them. If you have questions, and I'm sure you will, you can reread parts of the book or rewatch particular video clips. Ideally, you will be working with a group of colleagues, learning and implementing EIR together so that you can share successes and discuss questions and uncertainties together.

Grade 2 Basic EIR Procedures *(October–December)*

DAY 1 LESSON

1. Group rereads an "old" EIR story for fluency. Teacher conducts oral reading check or coaches in word recognition.

2. Teacher reads from "new" EIR book and models a variety of word-recognition strategies for three to five words from the story. Teacher discusses meanings of some unfamiliar words with students at point of contact in the story. Children reread story chorally.

3. Teacher coaches for comprehension and discusses meaning of other unfamiliar words not discussed in Step 2.

4. Group does Sound Box (October only) or Making Words activity.

DAY 2 LESSON

1. Group rereads an "old" story for fluency. Teacher conducts oral reading check or coaches in word recognition.

2. Group rereads "new" story twice with a partner or on their own while the teacher coaches individuals as needed.

3. Teacher coaches for comprehension.

4. Children write their own sentence about the story, based on a prompt provided by the teacher. Each child should be engaged in hearing the sounds in the words and in trying to write the letters for these sounds. They should be discouraged from copying words from the story (unless it is a name or other word that is difficult to spell). Each child shares his or her sentence with the teacher who points out one or two instances in which all of the sounds in a word are not represented or are in the wrong order.

DAY 3 LESSON

1. Group rereads an "old" story for fluency. Teacher conducts oral reading check or coaches in word recognition.

2. Group rereads "new" story twice with a partner or on their own while the teacher coaches as needed.

3. Teacher coaches for comprehension.

4. Individuals write a second sentence, based on a prompt provided by the teacher. Each child shares his or her sentence with the teacher who points out one or two instances in which all of the sounds in a word are not represented or are in the wrong order.

Figure 3-1 Grade 2 Basic EIR Procedures

Every day you and your group of five to seven children will reread old, or familiar, EIR stories (that is, those stories read in previous EIR lessons), read the current story, work on comprehension, and do word work or sentence writing. You need to pay careful attention to your timing to get through these four activities in 20 minutes (or 30 minutes at first). I always tell teachers that if they take longer than 20 to 25 minutes, they may be tempted to quit doing EIR because it seems to take up too much time.

Overview of the Lesson Steps

1. Group members reread stories they have read before in EIR lessons for fluency. Typically, the teacher gives them a number of the most recent books to reread and they select the ones they like the best. The teacher conducts an oral reading check with an individual or coaches in word recognition.

2. Teacher reads from a new book and models a variety of word-recognition strategies for three to five words from the story. The teacher discusses meanings of some unfamiliar words with students at point of contact in the story. Children reread story chorally.

3. Teacher coaches for comprehension and discusses meanings of other unfamiliar words not discussed in Step 2.

4. Teacher refines phonemic awareness and develops phonics knowledge with Sound Box or Making Words activity.

Day 1, Step 1: Reread Old Stories

(5 min.)

Take the first five minutes of the lesson to build children's confidence as they reread "old" stories by themselves or with a partner. You will work with one student on word recognition during this phase of the lesson. Rereading old stories gives the children the opportunity to experience fluent reading and success and helps them build their sight vocabulary. (See Chapter 4 for a list of the kinds of authentic literature children will be reading.)

Before students read with a partner, remind the children to give their partner a hint instead of telling the word. Since a major emphasis in EIR is on coaching children to be independent, you don't want a partner calling out a word when a child gets stuck. (Refer back to the examples of prompts students can use when partner reading.)

Examples of Prompts Students Can Give During Partner Reading

It starts with . . . (child gives his reading partner the beginning sound).

This part says . . . (child provides his partner with a rhyming part like *at* or *op*).

Look at the picture . . .

Look at this word again . . . (for child who misreads a word).

Prompts Teachers Can Use to Coach Students to Use Word-Recognition Strategies

Self-Monitoring Prompts

Good checking! How did you know it wasn't . . . ?

You said . . . . Does that make sense? Does that look and sound right?

Why did you stop? What did you notice?

Decoding Prompts

What can you do to figure out that word?

Is there a rhyming part you recognize?

Can you sound it out and come up with a word that makes sense?

Let's start again from the beginning of the sentence to see if this word makes sense.

What the Teacher Does

Use this rereading time to conduct an oral reading check (described in Chapter 7) with one child, coach a child who is having difficulty, or rotate among students in the group, listening to them read and coaching them in word recognition as needed. You can use the following prompts when coaching students to use word-recognition strategies.

see it in Action

video 1

DAY 1
Rereading Old Stories/ Assessing

On Day 1, second-grade teacher Kathy Arnold listens to students read their old stories and does oral reading checks. Kathy begins, "I'd like you to start reading books you know well. I'm going to do as many running records (oral reading checks) as I can." As she listens to a student read, she takes notes. At one point she asks, "How did you get this word?" The students says she looked at the /gr/ in *hungry*. The students are all very engaged in rereading old EIR stories.

Day 1, Step 2: Read New Story

(5 min.)

Read It Aloud

On Day 1 in October, it is important to read the new story to the children first so that you can track the words for them. Insist that their eyes are with you as you read, and stop on four to five words to model for the children different strategies for figuring out words. After you read the story to the children, read it again with them chiming in. You should briefly discuss the meaning of some potentially unfamiliar words as you are reading through the text for the first or second time.

ʃee it iN ActioN

Modeling Decoding Strategies

After reading the old story, Kathy reads the "newest" story, *The Happy Day* (Krauss 1989), with her group. First, she models strategies to use to figure out words. "I'm going to read a little, and I'm going to come to words and I might get stuck. You are going to help me." She comes to the phrase "field mice are sleeping" and says, "Feld, hmm, I need to look at the picture. I think I'll try /ee/, 'field mice are sleeping.'" When she comes to *snail* and reads *snall*, she says, "I see *ai*, I think I'll try /ay/—*snail.*" She continues to read and models different strategies for figuring out words. She uses the pictures for the word *squirrels* and notices the chunk *ound* in *ground*.

ʃee it iN ActioN

Choral Reading

Kathy and the group of six students then read the story chorally. "We're going to read *The Happy Day* together. Stay together like a chorus." Students track as they read with the teacher. Kathy stops them when they stumble on a word. "Let's go back to that page again." Students reread correctly this time. Students stumble on *ground* and a few come up with the word. Kathy asks, "How did you get *ground*?" Kai says, "I saw /ound/." Kathy coaches for others, "And what at the beginning? /gr/. You blended it together and got *ground*." Students continue to choral read. When they come to *sniff*, Kathy says, "Show me what sniff means. Everybody do it."

In Video 2, the teacher is modeling different strategies to figure out words as she was reading. This is an excellent technique to teach students to use multiple strategies when decoding. Often this part of the Day 1 routine gets skipped, but it is important to help make the notion of multiple word-recognition strategies concrete for the children. In Video 3, notice how deliberate the teacher is about asking the students about the strategies they used to figure out difficult words.

Day 1, Step 3: Coaching for Comprehension

(10 min.)

After decoding the story twice, take a few minutes to have students focus on the meaning of the story by asking a high-level question. (See the examples of questioning prompts in Figure 3-2.) So, what is a high-level question? It's one that gets the children to think about the story. It's not answered with yes or no. It can be one that prompts students to connect the meaning of the story to their own lives. Teachers who ask students to respond to high-level questions about what they have read see greater growth in students' reading scores than teachers who do less of this type of questioning (Taylor et al. 2003, 2005). Also take the time to briefly discuss potentially unfamiliar but high-utility words not discussed in Step 1.

ʃee it iN ActioN

video
4

Coaching for Comprehension

After reading the new story and coaching in word recognition in Step 2, Kathy asks students a high-level question about it. She asks them to summarize the story, something she is working on with the whole class. "What was important about the beginning of the story?" Students say, "The mouse is sleeping." Kathy elaborates, "All the animals are sleeping. What is happening in the middle?" One students says, "They start to run." Kathy coaches for more ideas, "And what else?" The student answers, "They sniff." Kathy asks, "How did the story end?" No one answers, so she coaches by showing students the last page. A student then adds, "The first flower grew." Kathy coaches, "What do you think is happening?" The boy says, "Spring is coming."

Kathy is very patient when asking her coaching questions, and it is useful to keep reminding yourself that wait time like this is important when asking children to express their thoughts. She also does an excellent job of coaching these ELL students to elaborate on their oral responses.

When you ask a thought-provoking comprehension question, you will not have time for all students to answer. Let one or two children answer, and explain to the others that you will call on them on Day 2 or Day 3.

Coaching for Comprehension
Questions and Prompts

The purpose of coaching for comprehension is to *expand* students' comprehension of what they have read rather than assess it. High-level questions are engaging, challenging, and require students to pause and think about before answering. When coaching you might:

▶ Stretch students' understanding of the story by asking them interpretive questions.

▶ Ask children to summarize all or part of the story or non-fiction text.

▶ Invite children to talk about the big idea, or theme, of the story.

▶ Ask children to relate the story to their own lives.

Examples of questions to coach for comprehension:

▶ What happened at the beginning of the story? The middle? The end? (Answer in just a few sentences.)

▶ Why did Character X do Y?

▶ How did Character X change?

▶ How are you like Character X? How are you different?

▶ What did you learn from this story?

▶ What did you like or not like about this story? Why?

Interpretive Questions Based on the Text

1. What kind of person do you think (name of character) is? What in the story makes you think this?

2. What are some good or bad things that happen in the story? Why do you think these are good or bad things?

3. What do you think is an important thing that happened in the story? Why do you think it is important?

4. How does (character in the story) compare to you or a family member? How is the character different?

5. Why do you think the author gave the title he or she did to the story?

6. What did you like best about (name a character)? Why? What in the story helped you think this way?

7. What did you not like about (name a character)? Why? What in the story made you think this way?

8. If you were the main character, would you have done the same things the main character did? Why or why not? What might you have done differently?

9. Why do you think (character in the story) did . . . ?

10. How did (character in the story) change? Why do you think this happened?

11. What do you think were three main ideas (or most important ideas) in this article (for nonfiction)?

High-Level Questions That Relate to Children's Lives

Ask questions that are based on a concept in the story or selection and relate it to children's lives.

1. Which character is most like you? Why?

2. Which character would you like to be like? Why?

3. Which character would you like to have as a friend? What in the story helped you make this decision?

4. How are you like (character in the story)? How are you different?

5. Can you compare anything in this story to (name another story or something else you have done in your classroom that could be compared)? Why do you think these are similar (alike) or different?

6. Ask nonfiction-type questions that relate to your state (e.g., Could you find these animals, events in Minnesota? Why or why not? Where might they be if they could be in Minnesota?).

7. What did you like about this story or nonfiction text? Why?

Figure 3-2 Coaching for Comprehension: Questions and Prompts

Day 1, Step 4: Phonemic Awareness and Phonics Work (Sound Box and Making Words Activities)

(5 min.)

The Sound Box Activity

Beginning in October, the Sound Box activity is the fourth step on Day 1 in Grade 2 for about a month; starting in November, the children will switch to the Making Words activity.

In the Sound Box activity, children are to write the letter or letters for one sound per box to focus on hearing the sounds in words. This activity helps students refine their phonemic awareness. As they gain skill with this activity, you should do less of the exaggerating of sounds for them and let them do this on their own, as needed. It is helpful for them if they say the actual word themselves. You may also want to ask them how many sounds they hear in a word, which will tell them how many boxes they will be using. To help students become more independent with sounding out words, post a short vowel chart in your small-group teaching area that shows vowels and pictures that begin with each short vowel sound, such as *a—apple, e—elephant, i—insect or i—igloo, o—octopus, u—umbrella* (see an example in Figure 3-3).

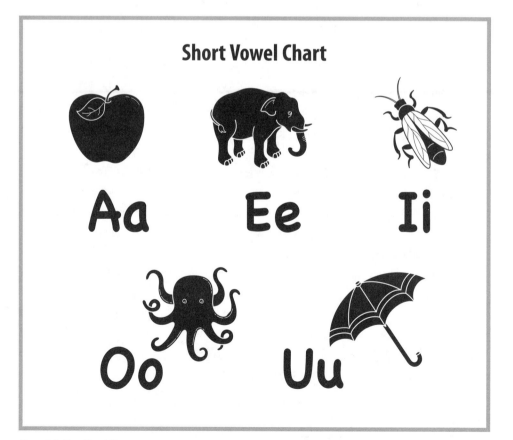

Figure 3-3 *Short Vowel Chart*

Also, you should introduce the advanced vowel chart (Figure 3-4) in the fall so that students can use it to help them as they write sound box words and write sentences about their EIR stories. You should regularly use the advanced vowel chart to support them and teach them to be flexible with their vowel sounds when they decode words they don't automatically recognize while

Advanced Vowel Chart

a	cat		cake	
e	hen		me	
i	pig		bike	
o	fox		rope	
u	bug		cube	
ea	bread		meat	
oo	school		book	
ow	cow		snow	
oa	boat			
oi	oil			
ee	feet			
ai	train			
ou	house			

Figure 3-4 Advanced Vowel Chart

reading EIR stories. The advanced vowel chart shows them common sounds for the same vowel (e.g., short and long *a*), or vowel team (e.g., the short *e*, long *e*, and long *a* sounds for *ea*). Although the long and short vowels are reviewed in early second-grade EIR lessons, vowel teams are the phonic elements to highlight in word work in second grade EIR lessons.

After writing the words in boxes, children should touch the words with their finger as they reread them. This helps students make the transition from hearing the sounds in words and writing the letters for these sounds to reading the words.

The words that are best for Sound Boxes depend on the children's development and what you are stressing in your regular reading program. For the most part, you should select words made up of three to five phonemes that have phonetically regular long or short vowel sounds represented by the CVC, CVCC, CVVC, or CVCE pattern (e.g., *hen*, *went*, *wait*, *time*). Once children are gaining skill in hearing the phonemes in words, you may want to add initial consonant blends (e.g., *pl*, *br*) or initial or final digraphs (e.g., *sh*, *ch*, *th*).

In Figure 3-5 you see words that would be good choices to use when reading *Show and Tell Sam* by Charnan Simon (1999). In *show* the *sh* would go together because these two letters make just one sound. If a child does not know that *ow* makes the long *o* sound in *show*, you can show them the *ow* and word *snow* on the advanced vowel chart. If a child can't tell what vowel is in the middle of *tell*, point to the short vowel chart and ask him, "Is it the sound you hear at the beginning of *apple*? Is it the sound you hear at the beginning of *elephant*? *insect*? *octopus*? *umbrella*?

Sound Boxes for *Show and Tell Sam*

1.	S	a	m	
2.	t	e	l	l
3.	b	e	s	t
4.	sh	ow		
5.	w	ai	t	

Figure 3-5 *Sound Boxes for* Show and Tell Sam

It often helps children hear the sounds the letters make if they say the words they are writing in a set of boxes. Also, it is important that children reread their sound box words to help them make the connection between the sounds they have heard in words and the words in print.

fee it iN ActioN

Sound Boxes

A first-grade teacher, Celia Huxley, hands out Sound Box sheets to the five students in her EIR group. As they start working on the first word, she says, "Listen carefully. Your job is to hear the sounds the words make and write the letters for them in the boxes. *Had.* What letter has the /h/ sound?" The students say "*h.*" The teacher continues, "What do you hear in the middle, /haaad/?" Students say, "/a/". "Write *a* in the second box. What do you hear at the end? /had/." Students say /d/. "Put your pencils down. Touch the letters like I do as we say the word. /h/, /a/, /d/, /had/." On the next word, *but,* the teacher reminds the students to say the word before they start writing. When the students give the letter name *u* for /u/, she reminds them about the short vowel chart. "/u/ sound like the *u* in *umbrella.*" At the end of the word, they again reread the sounds like they did with the first word, touching each letter as they say the sound for the letter, and then blending the sounds together: /b/, /u/, /t/, /but/. The teacher asks someone to use the word but in a sentence. Akouma says, "*I have a blanket, but my mom washed it.*" When they come to the word *made* and the teacher mentions the silent *e,* Jake shouts out that he has a silent *e* in his name. The teacher tells them to put the *e* after the *d* in the third box because they are putting one sound in a box and *e* is silent so it does not have its own box. When they come to the word *dress,* the teacher helps the students with the double *s* at the end of the word. "You don't hear it, but sometimes words have two *s's* at the end of the word." With the teacher, the students read all five words on their chart, sound by sound, and then they blend the sounds together. "You did an outstanding job. Give yourselves a hug." The teacher tells the students to take their Sound Box sheets home, read the words to someone at home, and make up a sentence for each word just like they did for the word *but.*

Making Words

Students enjoy the Sound Box activity, but beginning in November in second grade, it is typically more useful for them to switch to the Making Words activity for Step 4 on Day 1. In Making Words, which is based on the work of Pat Cunningham (2009), children are given letter squares that spell a "mystery word" from the story that is chosen by the teacher. The teacher tells them to take two or three letters to start with and make a particular word. Then the teacher tells them to add a letter, take away a letter, or rearrange letters to spell a different word. At the end of the activity the children are to use all of their letters to come up with the mystery word from the story. Additionally, students should use the short vowel chart to help them help them generate the correct short vowel. (See Figure 3-6 for a Making Words sequence for *George Shrinks* by William Joyce.)

ʃee it iN ActioN

video
6

Making Words

Kathy has students put the letter cards *w, i, n, r, g, g,* and *o* in alphabetical order. She tells them, "I'm going to give you a word and see if you can make it. *Win*. You can say it so you hear the beginning, middle, and end." Students say *win*. She coaches a student, Pai, who has spelled, *wing*. "Listen to the end, *win*." The student takes away the *g*. Kathy continues, "Pai knew the next word. Add one letter and make the word *wing*." A student proudly says, "I got the chunk *-ing*." Kathy coaches a student who is having trouble. Next, they make *ring*. "Take away one letter and add one to make *ring*. Slide your finger under the word as we read it. Put all your letters back. Make the word *now*." She breaks the words into /n/ /ow/ sounds. "What is the /ow/ sound? "After students make *now*, Kathy says, "Point to the two letters that say /ow/ so I know that you know." She has students make *gown*, say it, and read it. They then make *grow, row,* and *growing*. She praises students, "Good job! Give me five."

Making Words Sequences for *George Shrinks* by William Joyce

Pass out the following letter cards: *a, a, b, e, d, f, k, r, s, t*. Have students make the following words: *seat, beat, read, tear, fear, break, breakfast*. Say: Take four letters and make the word *seat*. Change one letter and make the word *beat*. Change two letters, and make the work *read*. Rearrange the letters you have to make the word *tear*. Change one letter and make the word *fear*. Take away one letter, add two letters, and make the word *break*. At the end, say, "Now take all of the letters to make the mystery word from the story" *(breakfast)*.

After Making Words, have students help you sort words (preprinted on cards) by word families: *seat, beat; tear, fear*. You could also talk about the fact that the sound in *read* could be the long *e* sound or the short *e* sound. Also, *ea* has the long sound of *a* in *break*.

Figure 3-6 Making Words Sequences for George Shrinks by William Joyce

As with Sound Boxes, a good strategy with Making Words is to have children say the words they are making since this will help them be more successful. The teacher in this example reminds the students to do this. She also has students slide their finger under each word as they read them before going on to the next word to make sure they are reading the word they just made.

Sorting Words as Part of Making Words

After children have done the Making Words activity, it is important to show them cards you have written that have the words they have made spelled out on them. You want students, one at a time, to tell you what words go together, whether this is by first letter or phonogram or by some other pattern. Often, children like to see if the other can guess how they sorted their words. It is important that you teach children how to sort by common phonograms and to talk to them about how in the future when they are reading, they may be able to figure out a hard word by recognizing the phonogram, or word chunk. For the exemplar book *George Shrinks* by William Joyce (1985), students would hopeful come up with *seat* and *beat*, for one word sort and *tear* and *fear* for another.

See it in Action

Word Sorting

Kathy puts cards on the table in front of the group of children. The words are the ones the students made during the Making Words activity. "Now I'm going to put all the words out and I want you to think, How can you put them together in some way?" The group reads the words. Francisco puts *growing* and *wing* together because of the *-ing* chunk. He puts *now, row,* and *grow* together. Kathy coaches, "Do all of the *-ow* words make the same sound?" She reads *now* and *row*. Students seem to think that they do. Kathy says, "How about this one, *gown,* should I put it with *now* or *row?*" Students say she should put it with *now*. Kathy talks to the students about how to transfer their knowledge of sounds for *ow* to words that contain *ow* when reading on their own. "You could try it both ways if you come to it in reading. How would you know which one? What makes sense? Does Kira have a *gone* (with long *o* sound) or a *gown?*" Students say *gown*. "When you read and come to *-ow* in a word, you can say /ow/ or /o/. Try both and see what makes sense."

The word sorts are an essential part of Making Words that often gets overlooked. You especially want the children to sort words by common phonograms. It is important to explain to the children, as the teacher did in the example, that learning to recognize common patterns, chunks, or phonograms will help them decode many words when they are reading on their own. I consistently recommend that teachers be explicit about how students can transfer to independent reading in this way. The teacher in the video clip does an excellent job of doing this with her students. She also does an excellent job of coaching as the students are sorting the words.

Pacing Tips

As you are following the basic second-grade procedures, it is important to remember to release responsibility to the children as soon as possible. I have found over the years, that as teachers, myself included, we tend to help children, especially those who are struggling, more than we should because we want them to be successful. You must continually ask yourself, "Is there something I am doing for the children that they can do for themselves?" It may be that you no longer need to exaggerate the sounds for them as they are writing words. Later in the year, you may not have to point out a specific word-recognition strategy to try because children will know several strategies to try themselves.

Also, keep in mind that you include all of the steps of the EIR program in the daily routine. At first, this may seem impossible, but teachers have found that they can do the EIR lesson in 20 minutes once they are familiar with the

PREPARING FOR MAKING WORDS SEQUENCES

▶ Start with words that follow the CVC or CVCe pattern at Level B. End with a word that is close in spelling to the mystery word, especially at Level B (e.g., *pig*, *piglet*). You can move into some sequences with vowel combinations if you feel your students are ready for this. For reinforcement, try to pick phonics elements that are being taught in your regular reading program at a similar point in time. Also see the scope and sequence for reinforcement of phonic elements in Table 4-3 in Chapter 4.

▶ As you are doing a Making Words sequence, notice from the examples that you typically should only change one letter each time. It is also a good idea to simply change the order of the letters, especially at Level B, so you can talk about how the order of the letters makes a difference (e.g., *was* versus *saw*).

▶ As you are preparing the sequences across stories, keep in mind that you want a variety of phonograms represented as opposed to using the same word family too often. For example, it would be better to select a mystery word for one story that features the *-ail* word family and for a second story a word from the *-eat* word family or from several word families. Repetition is fine, however, it is also important to expose children to many different word families. I mention this because I realize how much I think about this as I select mystery words for different stories. Selecting a good "mystery" word isn't that easy.

routine. Be aware of your pacing, however, so that you do not spend too much time on any one step. If you need to spend four days on a story at first, that is okay, but put pressure on yourself to reach the goal of getting through a story in three days. The basic second-grade procedures are summarized in Figure 3-1 so that you can refer to them easily as you first use them.

Helpful Resources
- A generic lesson planning form for EIR lessons (see Figure 4-1)
- Generic take-home activities (See Appendix 4-1)
- Vocabulary lists for exemplar books (see Appendix 4-2)
- Coaching for comprehension questions for exemplar books (See Appendix 4-3)
- Word lists to use in word work and sentence writing for exemplar books (see Appendix 4-4)
- Word lists for Making Words activities for exemplar books (see Appendix 4-5)

Summary of Day 1

As you can see, the four teaching steps for Day 1 are fairly straightforward. Nevertheless, you may want to reread the chapter and replay the video clips before you actually begin to teach Day 1. Also, after you have started to teach EIR lessons, by rereading the chapter, reviewing the videos, and discussing procedures with colleagues who are using EIR, you may notice points that you did not notice on your first reading that will help you be even more effective in your teaching. In the next section, we will cover the procedures for Days 2 and 3 of the three-day cycle.

Just as on Day 1, Day 2 has four components, or steps. You continue to work on the essential skills of word recognition, fluency, vocabulary, and comprehension, but you either focus on different students or you emphasize your teaching differently in one of the steps. In Step 1, as students reread old stories, they build their fluency and confidence as readers. You also get the chance to take a second oral reading check or coach a different student than you did the day before. As you reread the newest story in Step 2, you provide less support than you did on Day 1 because students now have some familiarity with reading the story. As you do less of the work for the students, they do more, and they build their confidence as readers. In Step 3, you ask a second question about the story that gets the children thinking and you get answers from different students than you did the previous day. In Step 4, you continue to build word-recognition abilities by having students engage in a different activity. This time, they write a sentence instead of doing Sound Boxes or Making Words.

Overview of the Lesson Steps

1. Group members reread stories from previous EIR lessons for fluency. Teacher conducts oral reading check or coaches in word recognition.

2. Group rereads "new" story twice with a partner or on their own while the teacher coaches individuals as needed.

3. Teacher coaches for comprehension.

4. Children write their own sentence about the story, based on a prompt provided by the teacher. Each child should be engaged in hearing the sounds in the words and in trying to write the letters for these sounds. They should be discouraged from copying words from the story (unless it is a name or other word that is difficult to spell). Each child shares his or her sentence with the teacher who points out one or two instances in which all of the sounds in a word are not represented or are in the wrong order.

Day 2, Step 1: Reread Old Stories

(5 min.)

The first step in the Day 2 routine is to have the children reread "old" stories by themselves or with a partner. During this time you should conduct an oral reading check, coach a child who is having trouble, or listen to a number of students read.

DAYS 2 and 3
Rereading

Kathy starts the EIR lesson by saying, "Choose a favorite book, and enjoy your reading. I'll just listen to you." She gets out of her seat to coach as she moves from one child to another. A boy gets stuck on *mile*, reading it as *mil*. "Look at this chunk, *ile*." The boy reads the word correctly. Kathy says, "Good readers start over, so let's start over to get the meaning of it."

Day 2, Step 2: Read the Newest Story

(5 min.)

Just as in Day 1, the second step of the Day 2 routine is to have the children reread the story twice. During the first reading in October, you may want to do a choral reading of the story, but if you do this, it is important that you let the children be the leading voice. Be sure your voice follows a little behind the children's voices. Also, continue to track for them until they are able to do this independently. Some students will still be unable to do this, but by consistently asking them to track and by coaching as needed, teachers find that most second-grade children in EIR are able to track in October if not before.

If students are reading chorally for this first reading, you need to coach as they get stuck on words. By November or December, you should omit the choral reading and have the students read the story with a partner and then on their own. As children read to a partner or to themselves, they should each have their own copy of the story to read. As they are reading on their own or with a partner, you can listen to and coach individuals. As you coach in word recognition, remember to use the advance vowel chart. For example if a student gets stuck on the vowel sound when reading the word 'flower', show him the two words next to *ow, cow* and *snow*. Ask, which sound for *ow* would make more sense in this word, the sound you hear for *ow* in *cow* or the sound you hear for *ow* in *snow?*

See it in Action

Partner Reading

Students read the newest story twice with a partner on Day 2 as Kathy listens to pairs of students read. At this point, they should track as they read. A little later in the year, they will no longer need to track when this seems to slow them down or makes them read in a choppy manner. Kathy begins, *"We are going to read the book we read yesterday. You are going to be partner reading. What do you do if your partner comes to a word they don't know?"* Students offer suggestions, *Give a chunk, sound it out, tell them to look at the picture. Ask Does it make sense?* Kathy explains to students that one student reads two pages, then the other reads two pages. Then they start at the beginning and switch who reads first. Moving around the table, Kathy listens to students read and coaches as they stumble on words.

Remind students to use a variety of different prompts to figure out words. Sometimes teachers tend to stress the same prompt, such as, "Sound it out," but this doesn't communicate to the children that there are a number of strategies that they can use to figure out a word they don't know. Also, if a child pauses on a word and gets the word right or if the child self-corrects a word, you can praise the child and ask the child to explain what he did to figure out the word. By doing this, you are helping children become aware of their metacognitive and self-monitoring efforts.

Coaching prompts that you use include questions that get the children to reflect on what they are doing (self-monitoring prompts) as well as questions that get them to try one or more word-attack strategies (decoding prompts) are listed on page 43. You may want to look at the variety of your coaching prompts when you watch a video of yourself teaching EIR lessons.

Children in second grade will typically attempt to use sequential decoding right away in the fall. This is just something that they did not quite master in first grade 1. However, is it good to model decoding by onset and rime for second-grade EIR students in the fall so that it will be a familiar strategy that children will start to try on their own later as the school year progresses.

Day 2, Step 3: Coaching for Comprehension

(10 min.)

Before you move on to sentence writing, you again talk about the story and coach for comprehension. Just as you did on Day 1, ask one question about the story that gets the children to think, or you ask them to relate the story to their lives, again posing a question that gets the children to think. Since not everyone can answer every day, be sure to call on children you didn't call on during Day

ſee it iN ActioN

Coaching for Comprehension

Kathy says, "I want you to think about how the animals feel at this point." She shows them the last page of the story as animals are sniffing the flower. A student says, "They feel happy." Kathy coaches the student to elaborate by asking, "Why?" The student adds, "It is spring and it's growing." Kathy continues, "Now think about you. If you saw signs of spring, how would you feel?" Students offer ideas. "I would feel happy. I could go swimming, I could ride a bike." Kathy tells students she wants them to write about their idea for sentence writing.

After students make connections to the story, the teacher follows up by having students use their ideas in Step 4, Sentence Writing. In this way, she makes the sentence writing a comprehension as well as a phonics and writing-for-sounds activity.

Day 2, Step 4: Sentence Writing

(5 min.)

The fourth step on Day 2 is sentence writing. In second grade, it is important that each child try to write his or her own sentence, say each word, listen for the sounds in sequence, and write letters that go with these sounds. The teacher gives the group a prompt and each child writes her own sentence in response to this prompt. The children use approximate, or invented, spelling. Once children finish their sentence, they share it with the teacher. She does not correct all misspelled words but helps each child with one or two words to refine the child's phonemic awareness and phonics knowledge.

Consider the sentence, *I brush my teeth and listen to a story.* Students might write this sentence after reading *Ten, Nine, Eight* by Molly Bang (1996). Although you want the children to do as much of the writing themselves as possible, if there are sounds that the children don't know how to spell correctly, such as the *ee* in *teeth* or silent letters such as the *t* in *listen*, you should simply tell the children the letters for these sounds. If children get stuck on a short vowel sound that is spelled with a single letter, such as the *u* in *brush*, don't just tell them the letter but instead, help them learn to use the short vowel chart to figure out how to spell a particular short vowel sound. For example, help them figure out that the second sound in *bus* is the sound that is heard at the beginning of *umbrella*. It is important to keep the short vowel chart, and advanced vowel chart, with you as you teach. See Figure 3-2 for the kinds of questions that could be used for sentence prompts. Also see sentence prompts for exemplar books in Appendix 4-3 on the DVD.

ʃee it iN ActioN

video
11

Sentence Writing

Kathy makes sure that every child has an idea before they write about how they would feel and what they would do if they saw signs of spring. One boy says, "I could use my skateboard again." One girl says, "I could see the flowers grow."

Kathy moves around to see what students are writing. She has them read their sentences to her. To refine their phonemic awareness and phonics knowledge, she coaches them on one or two words in which letters do not represent the correct sounds or letters for sounds are in the wrong order. One student writes, I *fel like the flowr and the sun is very warm.* Kathy coaches her on *feel*. "Does *fel* look right? What should it have? Yes, it should have two *e's."* She also helps with the word *flower*. "Do you know what often goes with *r* at the end of a word?" The student comes up with *er*. Another student writes, I *would be happy if a saw a spring flower.* Kathy coaches this student on putting /ow/ in /flower/. "Can you remember what letters made the /ow/ sound when we were working on word sorts?" The child comes up with *ow.*

The teacher in this example does an excellent job of coaching as the students are writing. She praises them for looking at the word wall. Also, she does not just give them correct spellings. Since one of the purposes of the sentence writing is to refine children's phonemic awareness, the teacher should point out a word or two in which all of the sounds are not represented, as the *er* in *flower* in the video clip or the sounds are not represented in the correct order, just as in *fro* instead of *for*.

Summary of Day 2

Day 2 reinforces and deepens students' understandings from Day 1 by increasing their fluency with repeated readings, extending their word recognition through additional opportunities to read with the teacher, as well as expanding their comprehension with further questions and sentence writing.

Day 3
Lesson Routine

The routine on Day 3 is almost the same as on Day 2. The biggest difference is that the children are able to do things with less help than they were on Day 2. Your students contribute with greater independence now because the practice and consistent structure combines to help them feel more confident and capable as readers.

Overview of the Lesson Steps

1. Group rereads old story for fluency. Teacher conducts oral reading check or coaches in word recognition.

2. Group rereads new story twice with a partner or on their own while the teacher coaches as needed.

3. Teacher coaches for comprehension.

4. Individuals write a second sentence, based on a prompt provided by the teacher. Each child shares his or her sentence with the teacher who points out one or two instances in which all of the sounds in a word are not represented or are in the wrong order.

Day 3, Step 1: Reread Old Stories

(5 min.)

Like Days 1 and 2, the first step in the Day 3 routine is to have the children reread old stories by themselves or with a partner as you conduct an oral reading check or coach a child who is having trouble. Of course, it is important to get around to all of the children and coach as they read, but you will find that since there are numerous opportunities for coaching built in to the EIR model, you can especially focus on those children who are most in need of your help.

Day 3, Step 2: Read Newest Story

(5 min.)

The second step of the Day 3 routine is to have the children reread the newest story twice. Children read to a partner and then silently to themselves. As children are reading on their own or with a partner, you can listen to and coach individuals. If they need help with a short vowel sound, have them use the short vowel chart. If they are having trouble with a vowel team, use the advanced vowel chart.

As children read with a partner, it is important to remind them to not shout out a word when a partner gets stuck, but to instead give a hint. We have found it helpful to give children a few things to say when a partner gets stuck. They will need constant, gentle reminding, however, to use these prompts. (See prompts for partner reading on page 43.)

Day 3, Step 3: Coaching for Comprehension

(5 min.)

Before you move on to sentence writing, you coach for comprehension. Again, you ask a high-level question about the story, or have the children relate the story to their own lives. Since not everyone can answer everyday, be sure to call on children you didn't call on during Days 1 or 2.

Day 3, Step 4: Sentence Writing

(5 min.)

The fourth step, as in Day 2, is sentence writing. Students continue to write individual sentences in response to a teacher prompt. By December or January, you can give students a number of question prompts, such as questions from Figure 3-2. Choose a question and write a sentence or two to answer your question about the story. Remind them not to copy from the book. They can share writing ideas with a partner or the teacher before they begin to write. After they have written their sentences, they share it with the teacher. She does not correct all misspelled words, but helps each child correctly spell one or two words to refine their phonemic awareness and phonics knowledge.

Summary of Day 3

As you can see, the four teaching steps for Days 1, 2, and 3 build on one another to strengthen students' confidence and abilities as they learn to read. Typically by January, or sooner, many second graders are ready to read books with less teacher support. This phase of EIR is called the transition phase, which is discussed in Chapter 5.

Daily Opportunity for One-on-One Reading Practice with a Coach

In addition to working with the teacher daily in a small group, each child also needs the opportunity every day to reread their current EIR story (or an old, familiar EIR story if they have not yet read the new story with the teacher) to someone who has been taught how to coach as the child is reading. This person may be an educational assistant, a volunteer, or an older student. In Chapter 9, I provide suggestions for the training of one-on-one coaches.

It should only take about five to seven minutes for a child to read her EIR story to a coach. In addition to knowing how to coach on easier words, a coach needs to be trained in how to help on hard words if a child is getting frustrated, or sometimes just telling a child a word if necessary.

One-on-one coaching is an essential part of EIR that often gets overlooked. It may be difficult to find people to do the one-on-one coaching, but children make rapid progress when this important piece is in place.

At the same time as I mention the value of one-on-one coaching, I want to stress the point that I do not believe the EIR small group should be taught by anyone but a licensed teacher. Children who are having trouble learning to read need quality instruction from those who have the most expertise.

If adults are not available to do the one-on-one coaching, we have found that children a few years older than the second-grade EIR students can be taught to do a reasonably good job of coaching. Teachers have found that this cross-age tutoring, described in *Catching Readers*, Grade 4/5 (Taylor forthcoming), not only helps the younger students improve in reading, but also helps the third, fourth, or fifth graders improve in reading as well as in their concepts about themselves as readers (Taylor et al. 1997).

4

Book Selection Guides and Other Lesson-Planning Resources

● ●

Providing students with quality children's literature to read is an essential piece of effective instruction, and every EIR lesson relies on an engaging book. Too often struggling readers are given materials that hinder their achievement—dull texts written to drill skills rather than engage young readers in meaningful stories and nonfiction. In this chapter, I give you guidance on how to select high quality, engaging books that fit the EIR model. However, I want to emphasize that you need to make their own choices and discoveries about the fiction and nonfiction books to use in EIR lessons. Why? Because following someone else's suggestions somehow flattens the vitality of the teaching and learning. Go with your own expertise and interests, as well as the curiosities and sense of humor of your students.

In this chapter, you will find charts that will help you know the characteristics to look for when choosing books for EIR as well as sample lists that will

help you use these books to plan and carry out the four lesson steps. You'll see lists on comprehension, vocabulary, phonics, and word making/sorting activities. In the spirit of cheerleading you, two I want to highlight now are: the general lesson-planning template (Figure 4-1) and the sample reading at home sheet (Figure 4-2). Both resources have a comforting structure that you'll get used to quickly. And do not forget the importance of encouraging parents/caregivers to instill good reading habits in their second graders!

See the DVD for full-size versions of all the forms in this chapter.

Generic Lesson-Planning Form

Sound Box or Making Words	**Coaching for comprehension questions for Days 1, 2, and 3** (List the questions to ask children.)

Oral Reading Check results and notes for following children:	

Notes

Take-Home Activity (Notes regarding take-home activity)	**Oral Reading Check/Oral Reading Analysis** (List children)

Figure 4-1 *Generic Lesson-Planning Form*

Reading at Home

Date _____

_____ **has read the book**
(student's name)

_____ **to me** _____ **times.**
(book title)

Comments: _____

_____

_____

_____

_____

_____

_____

_____

_____
(parent's/caregiver's signature)

Figure 4-2 Reading at Home Sheet

Grade 2 Books: What to Look For

Books for grade 2 are divided into seven levels that cover pre-primer 1, pre-primer 2, primer, end of grade 1, first half of grade 2, and second half of grade 2 (for accelerated grade 2 model). I call them EIR levels in this book so they aren't confused with Guided Reading Levels (Fountas and Pinnell 1996).

In second grade, you will need only 2 or 3 books at Level A, and 5 to 6 books at each of the EIR Levels B, C, D, E, and F. You will also need from 5–6 narrative and 5–6 informational books for the Accelerated Model (see Table 4-1). The number of books you will need at each level will vary, depending on the reading abilities of your students. Also you will spend more than one week on the books at Level F, and for the Accelerated Model. Examples of suitable books for the EIR model are shown in Table 4-2. In addition to quality children's literature, there are some leveled book series from major publishing houses that you can select texts from as well, including Step Into Reading, All Aboard Reading, and I Can Read. The important thing is that students find the books engaging so that they're motivated to work hard at learning to read. Guidelines to help you select books are provided on page 69 and a scope and sequence of phonic elements to focus upon in EIR lessons at different EIR book levels are in Table 4-3.

Characteristics of Grade 2 Books at Different EIR Levels

Grade 2 EIR Level	Traditional Reading Level	Guided Reading Level*	Length (words)	Time to Use
Level A	PP	D E	40–60	Oct.
Level B	PP-P	F G	60–90	Nov.–Dec.
Level C (use with Level E)	P-1²	G H I	90–120	Jan.–Feb.
Level D (use with Level F)	2¹	J K	120–200	March
Level E	P1² (e.g., Step into Reading I Can Read Level 1)	F G H	—	Jan.–Feb.
Level F	1² 2¹ (e.g., I Can Read Level 2)	I J K	—	Mar.–May
Accelerated	2²	L M		

From Fountas and Pinnell (1996), Guided Reading. Portsmouth, NH: Heinemann.

Table 4-1 Characteristics of Grade 2 Books at Different EIR Levels

Examples of Grade 2 Books

EIR Level	Book Title	Author
A: 40–60 words	*Flying* *Show and Tell Sam*	Donald Crews Charnan Simon
B: 60–90 words	*The Cake That Mack Ate* *The Lady with the Alligator Purse* *Rain* *Cookie's Week* *George Shrinks*	Rose Robart Nadine Bernard Wescott Robert Karlan Cindy Ward William Joyce
C: 90–120 words (alternate with Level E)	*Dinosaurs, Dinosaurs* *Sheep on a Ship* *Ten, Nine, Eight* *Who Is the Beast?* *A Hat for Minerva Louise*	Byron Barton Nancy Shaw Molly Bang Keith Baker Janet Morgan Stoeke

D: 100–200 words
(alternate with
Level F)
	Animals Should Definitely
	  Not Wear Clothing
	The Little Mouse, the Red Ripe
	  Strawberry, and the Big Hungry Bear
	Milton the Early Riser
	Mr. Gumpy's Outing
	What Game Shall We Play?
		Judi Barrett
		
		Don and Audrey Wood
		
		Robert Kraus
		John Burningham
		Pat Hutchins

E: Easy Readers
(alternate with
Level C)
	Five Silly Fisherman
	My New Boy
	Ready? Set. Raymond!
	What a Hungry Puppy
	Also: Step Into Reading, Step 2,
	  Random House; All Aboard Reading,
	  Level 1, Grosset & Dunlap;
	  Hello Reading, Viking;
	  I Can Read Level 1, Harper Collins
		R. Edwards
		Joan Phillips
		Vaundra Micheaux Nelson
		Gail Herman

F: Easy Readers
(alternate with
Level D)
	Four on the Shore
	Fox All Week
	Frog and Toad Together
	There Is a Carrot in My Ear
	  and Other Noodle Tales
	Three By the Sea
	Also: I Can Read Level 2, Harper Collins,
	  or other easy readers at comparable level
		Edward Marshall
		Edward Marshall
		Arnold Lobel
		Alvin Schwartz
		
		Edward Marshall

continues

Table 4-2 *Examples of Grade 2 Books*

Examples of Grade 2 Books, *continued*

EIR Level	Book Title	Author
Accelerated Books Fiction	*The Salamander Room* *Good Driving, Amelia Bedelia* *Tacky the Penguin* *The Stories Huey Tells* *Tornado* Also: I Can Read, Levels 2–3, Harper Collins; Stepping Stone Books, Random House and other series books at comparable levels	Anne Mazer Peggy Parish Helen Lester Anne Cameron Betsy Byars
Accelerated Books Non-fiction	*Harry Houdini, Escape Artist* *Wolves* *Ears* (Animal Parts) *Great Lakes* *Helen Keller and the Big Storm* *Let's Go Rock Collecting* Also: I Can Read, Levels 2–3, Scholastic Science Readers, Levels 2; Ready-to-Read, Level 2, Simon & Schuster; Stepping Stone Books, Random House and other series books at comparable levels	Patricia Lakin Carolyn Otto Elizabeth Miles Kimberley Valzania Patricia Lakin Roma Gans

Table 4-2 Examples of Grade 2 Books, continued

GUIDELINES FOR SELECTING GRADE 2 EIR BOOKS

1. Reading selections should follow the length guidelines for EIR Levels A, B, C, and D that are in Table 4-1. If you want to use a book at a particular level but it is too long, have the children only read part of the selection over the 3-day cycle and then read another part over a second 3-day cycle.

2. Make sure a story is interesting enough that you can spend 3 days on it; the children should still enjoy it at the end of 3 days. Also, you need to be able to ask higher-level questions on the story for 3 days.

3. At EIR Level A you do not want a story to be so predictable that a child can read it "with his eyes shut." In a story such as the following, children can "read" the text by looking at the pictures instead of the words, "One black dog runs, two white rabbits hop, three red birds sing, etc." Instead, in EIR lessons we want children's eyes to "glue to the print."

4. At EIR Levels A-E, there should be enough CVC (or permutations of CCVCC), CVCe (or CCVCe), and CVVC (or CCVVC), words in texts that a child can practice letter-by-letter sequential decoding and decoding by onset and rime as well as apply their phonics knowledge to words they are decoding. See the scope and sequence of suggested phonic elements to stress at different EIR levels in Table 4-3.

5. Since three days are spent on a story and you want your students to be motivated, the texts should be fun to read. Many leveled readers may not be engaging enough, however, so you need to select them carefully.

Suggested Scope and Sequence of Phonic Elements to Focus on During Decoding Instruction

Grade 2 Overview

Level A	Level B	Level C	Level D	Level E	Level F
ai	ea	ea	ou	oy	wr
ow	ur		aw		
	oi				
	oa				
	ir				

Grade 1 Overview

Level A	Level B	Level C	Level D		
short a	short e	sp	cl		
short i	cvc-e	sl	pr		
short u	ee	sw	dr		
short o	ai	sn	sc		
	ar		ch		
	gr	th	wh		
	gl	er	qu		
	st	ay	ea		
	cr	ing	oo		
	sm	ir	ow		
	br		ou		
	fl		y = long i		
	sh				
	ck				

Table 4-3 Suggested Scope and Sequence of Phonic Elements to Focus on During Decoding Instruction

Book-Related Resources to Help You Plan Lessons

Remember, you do not need to use the particular books that are listed here. Use them as exemplars to get you started, along with the sample support material that follows. What is important is that you understand what words for word work to focus upon with the leveled books you choose to use for EIR lessons (see Table 4-3). Additional resources that will help you teach EIR lessons are available on the DVD. Materials include teaching charts; generic take-home activities for the children to use with their EIR stories (Appendix 4-1); a list of exemplar EIR books (also see Table 4-2); and for exemplar books, vocabulary to focus upon, questions to use when coaching for comprehension or for sentence writing prompts, words to use in sound boxes and sentence writing, words for making words activities, and lesson-planning forms and independent activities for exemplar transition books (see Appendices 4-2 to 4-6). There are also assessment directions and recording forms (see Chapter 7). All of these materials are provided full size on the DVD so you can print them out as needed.

Take-Home Activities/Level A

Story Title: _____

Student Name: _____   Parent Signature: _____

Choose words from the story. Write the word on the line and draw a picture of that word.

Choose your word.   Draw a picture.   Write it again.

See Appendix 4-1 Generic Take-Home Activities

Examples of Vocabulary to Discuss in Exemplar Grade 2 Books

Please Note: These are only suggested words to talk about in terms of meaning at point of contact in the stories. Teachers should make choices based on their students' needs. I want to thank the elementary and ELL teachers who helped create these lists. For some of these books, there are no words to suggest for all students as vocabulary—that is, words whose meanings they do not know.

Books	Possibilities for All Students	Possibilities for ELLs
Level A		
Flying	*boarding, taxiing*	*cities, country, mountains*
Show and Tell Sam	*shortcut*	*sharpen*
Level B		
The Cake That Mack Ate	*lit*	*farmer, candles, married*
The Lady with the Alligator Purse	*nonsense, penicillin*	*purse, throat*
Rain		*fence*
Cookie's Week		*week, garbage, tomorrow*
George Shrinks		*check, dreamt, shrinks, note*
Level C		
Dinosaurs, Dinosaurs	*armored plates, fierce, spikes*	*dinosaurs, sharp, sails*
Sheep on a Ship	*collide, raft*	*waves, storm, map, nap, trip*
Ten, Nine, Eight	*pale, windowpanes, gown*	*straight, fuzzy*
Who Is the Beast?	*beast, whiskers, tracks*	*fear, sight*
A Hat for Minerva Louise	*exploring*	*fluffy*
Level D		
Animals Should Definitely Not Wear Clothing	*disastrous, unnecessary, manage, embarrassing*	*lose, messy, mistake*
The Little Mouse, the Red Ripe Strawberry, and the Big Hungry Bear	*especially, tromp, disguised*	*guarding, share, half*
Mr. Gumpy's Outing	*squabble, trample*	*owned, tease, fields*
What Game Should We Play?	*field*	*hide and seek*
Level E		
Five Silly Fisherman	*dock*	*fine*
My New Boy		*scratch, lucky*
		sneakers, chew, rush
		smelly

See Appendix 4-2 Examples of Vocabulary to Discuss in Exemplar Grade 2 Books

---

Questions or Sentence-Writing Prompts for Exemplar Grade 2 Stories

Please Note: These are only examples. You may wish to come up with your own questions.

Level A

Flying
▶ Would you like to go on an airplane? Why or why not?
▶ Have you ever been to the airport? What did you like?
▶ Where would you like to go on a plane? Why?

Level B

The Cake That Mack Ate
▶ How did you feel about the ending? Why?
▶ Whose birthday do you think it was?
▶ What do you like about birthdays?

Lady with the Alligator Purse
▶ Write a sentence about something in the story that couldn't really happen.
▶ What was a part of the story that you thought was funny?
▶ Tell about something funny that happened to you or someone in your family.

Rain
▶ What did you like about this book?
▶ What do you like about a rainy day?

George Shrinks
▶ If you were as little as George, what would you like to do?
▶ Tell about a picture you like in the book and why.
▶ What would happen to George if he were as big as a giant?

Level C

Ten, Nine, Eight
▶ What do you do to get ready for bed?
▶ Tell about a favorite page or picture.

Who Is the Beast?
▶ What picture do you like? Why?
▶ Who do you think the beast is in the story?

A Hat for Minerva Louise
▶ What did you like about this book?
▶ Have you ever lost your mittens? Tell us about it.

Level D

Animals Should Definitely Not Wear Clothing
▶ Animals should not wear clothing because . . .
▶ Animals should not _____ because_____ . . .

The Little Mouse, the Red Ripe Strawberry, and the Big Hungry Bear
▶ What is Mouse's problem and how does he solve it?
▶ Where or how would you have hidden the strawberry?
▶ How do you hide something you don't want someone to see?

Mr. Gumpy's Outing
▶ How do you feel about the ending? Why?
▶ Have you ever gone for a boat ride? Tell us about it.
▶ How is this story like *The Mitten*?

What Game Shall We Play?
▶ What game were the animals playing?
▶ Where is a good hiding place when you play hide-and-seek?
▶ Tell about a time you have played hide-and-seek and who you played with.

See Appendix 4-3 Questions or Sentence Writing Prompts for Exemplar

Examples of Words to Focus on During Decoding Instruction or Sentence Writing for Exemplar Grade 2 Books

GRADE 2/LEVEL A

Introduction	Choices for Review	Book Name	Words to Focus on During Decoding Instruction or Sentence Writing
Level A			
	ing	*Flying*	*flying, taxiing*
	er		*rivers, over*
	ay		*highways, runway*
	y=e		*ready, country*
ai		*Show and Tell Sam*	*paint, wait*
ow			*how, show, showed*
	short i		*him, it, still, misses*
	short a		*Sam, snack, class*
	short e		*tell, best*
	short o		*dog*
	short u		*much*

GRADE 2/LEVEL B

Introduction	Choices for Review	Book Name	Words to Focus on During Decoding Instruction or Sentence Writing
Level B			
	cvc-e	*The Cake That Mack Ate*	*ate, cake*
	short e		*hen, fed, egg*
	th		*that, this*
ur		*The Lady with the Alligator Purse*	*purse, nurse*
oi			*oil*
*oa			*soap, boat, throat*
*ea			*eat, measles*
	ow	*Rain*	*flowers, yellow, brown, rainbow*
	*oa		*road*
oi		*Cookie's Week*	*toilet*
ir			*dirt*
	ar		*garbage*
	oo		*cookie*
	ur		*curtains*
*ea		*George Shrinks*	*eat, clean, please*
	ai		*mail*

*ea can be introduced and/or reviewed in *George Shrinks* and *The Lady with the Alligator Purse* in Level B or in *Ten Nine Eight* and *A Hat for Minerva Louise* in Level C.

*oa can be introduced and/or reviewed in *The Lady with the Alligator Purse* or *Rain*.

continues

See Appendix 4-4 Examples of Words to Focus on During Decoding Instruction or Sentence Writing for Exemplar Books

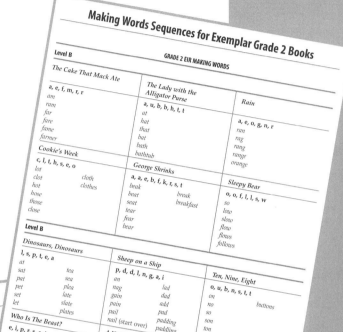

Making Words Sequences for Exemplar Grade 2 Books

Level B

GRADE 2 EIR MAKING WORDS

The Cake That Mack Ate

a, e, f, m, r, r
am
ram
far
fare
fame
farmer

The Lady with the Alligator Purse

a, u, b, b, h, t, t
at
hat
that
bat
bath
bathtub

Rain

a, e, o, g, n, r
ran
rag
rang
range
orange

Cookie's Week

c, l, t, h, s, e, o
lot
clot   cloth
hot   clothes
hose
those
close

George Shrinks

a, a, e, b, f, k, r, s, t
beak
beat   break
seat   breakfast
tear
fear
bear

Sleepy Bear

o, o, f, l, l, s, w
so
low
slow
flow
flows
follows

Level B

Dinosaurs, Dinosaurs

l, s, p, t, e, a
at
sat   tea
pat   sea
pet   plea
set   late
let   slate
              plates

Sheep on a Ship

p, d, d, l, n, g, a, i
an
nag   lad
gain   dad
pain   add
pail   pad
nail (start over)   padding
                    paddling

Ten, Nine, Eight

o, u, b, n, s, t, t
on
no   buttons
so
son
ton
but

Who Is The Beast?

e, i, p, r, s, s, t
tip
sip   trips
sir   stripe
rip   stripes
ripe
trip

A Hat for Minerva Louise

g, i, m, n, n, o, r, s
or
no   grin
nor   ring
morn (start over)   sing
more   mornings
in

continues

Level E/Lesson Planner

Five Silly Fishermen

Coaching for comprehension questions (List the questions to ask children.)

Independent Activities (Optional)

Writing Prompts
1. Have you ever gone fishing? Tell us about it.
2. Why are they called five *silly* fishermen in the story?

Summarize this book in three sentences. The first sentence is done for you.
1. The five fishermen each caught a fish.
2. Write a sentence about the mistake the fisherman made.
3. Write a sentence about how the little girl tricked the men.

Making Words
a, e, i, k, m, s, t
mist
mast
mate
make
take
sake
stake
mistake

Word Families
Write other words that end like *found*.
pound
sound
hound
bound
ground

Take-Home Activity
(Notes regarding activity)

Oral Reading Check/Oral Reading Analysis
(List children)

See Appendix 4-5 Making Words for Exemplar Grade 2 Books

See Appendix 4-6 Lesson Planner

5

The Transition Phase

Helping Second Graders Read Independently

Typically, by January in second grade, or earlier if students are ready, you'll shift to the transition phase of EIR. You base this shift on students' oral reading check scores (see Chapter 7) and, of course, your own knowledge of each young reader. The hallmark of this phase is that you're coaching children as they read a book *they have never read before* in an EIR lesson.

All year long, your second graders who entered second grade not yet reading independently at a first-grade level and who are in EIR have been "reading" books on their own at the emergent reading level (e.g., Guided Reading Levels A–C, Fountas and Pinnell 1996), looking at many other books in the room, and rereading books from their guided reading group lessons. Much of this independent reading transpires during the independent work time of the reading block. The difference now is that you bring independent reading of books students have never read before into the EIR lesson itself with books at a first-grade level (e.g., EIR Level E or Guided Reading Levels F–H) and a end of first to second-grade level (e.g., EIR Level F or Guided Reading Levels I–K). Until now, you've been using EIR repeated reading procedures with books at EIR

Levels A–B that correspond to Guided Reading Levels D–G with those students who entered second grade not yet reading. Your goal is to get children reading independently for sustained periods as soon as possible on a second-grade level (e.g., Guided Reading levels K–L or higher). Once they can really read on their own, they need to practice reading as much as possible. Hopefully, they will then be reading on grade level by the end of the year.

Another purpose of the transition phase is to have children leave school for the summer feeling confident about their ability to read independently so they will continue to read over the summer. In the teacher resources on the DVD that comes with this book, there is a suggested summer reading list that illustrates the types of books that would be a good level for EIR students at the end of grade 2 to read.

The transition reading procedures that are detailed in this chapter and summarized in Figure 5-1 are used with all of the books at EIR Levels E and F in grade 2 (also see Tables 4-1 and 4-2 in Chapter 4).

When Are Students Ready?

In writing this book, I wrestled with where to put the assessment chapter. I decided I wanted to give you all the lesson cycle routines before going into detail about which children benefit from EIR, the assessments involved, and how you know children are ready for the midyear transition. Flip ahead to Chapter 7 if you want to take a glance at the assessments, but for now, remember the following two rules of thumb:

1. If students are able to read books they have never seen before that are at a mid-first-grade level (e.g., Guided Reading Levels F–G) with at least 92 percent accuracy in word recognition, they are ready to begin with the transition procedures and books at EIR Level E (e.g., Guided Reading Levels F–H).

2. If your students are able to read books they have never read before that are at an end-of-first-grade level (e.g., Guided Reading Levels H–I with a least 92 percent accuracy in word recognition, then they are ready to read transition books at EIR Level.F (Guided Reading Levels I–K) in EIR lessons.

IF YOU STARTED EIR MIDYEAR

If you started the intervention in February, you most likely began with the three-day repeated reading cycle with several EIR Level D books to build up students' confidence (Remember, reading a book through the repeated reading cycle is easier than reading the same book "cold.") However, if students are able to read books *they have never seen before* that are at an end-of-first-grade level, (e.g., Guided Reading Levels H–I) with at least 93 percent accuracy in word recognition, then they are ready to begin with the transition books at EIR Level F (e.g., Guided Reading Levels I–K).

February–May: How the Three-Day Routine Changes

With books from EIR Levels E and F during the transition phase, you no longer work with all of the children in a group at once but instead read with just two children at a time. After you have read with two children, they should read their story to their partner, to themselves, and to their coach. The other students in the EIR group reread favorite books, read new books, and complete open-ended response activities related to the books they have read. In Chapter 8, I describe a number of motivating, independent activities for children as they are interacting with texts, and I offer open-ended response sheets for these activities as well. Also, on the lesson planners for exemplar transition books (see Appendix 4-6) on the DVD, there are useful independent activities children can work on while you work with other pairs in the EIR group.

Small-Group and Transition Reading Rotation for Levels C and E (January–February) and D and F (March–May)

▶ **Days 1–3:** Read a Level C book (such as the examples in the small-group book list in Table 4-2 in Chapter 4) following the regular three-day format with the group of students. (See Figure 3-1.)

▶ **Days 4–6:** Select a Level E book (such as the examples in the transition book list to be used with the transition reading steps that appear in Figure 5-1).

▶ **Days 7–9:** Now go back to reading a Level C book (such as the examples in the small-group book list following the basic three-day repeated reading format with the group).

▶ **Days 10–12:** For the next three-day cycle, select a Level E book (such as the examples in the transition book list) to use with the transition procedures.

Continue rotating between the three-day repeated reading and transition process until all Level C and E books are completed. For grade 2 Levels D and F, continue alternating between Level D books using the three-day repeated reading process and Level F books using the transition process until all Level D books are gone. Then continue with Level F books for the remainder of the year.

Transition to Independent Reading

Instructional Procedures for Levels C and E (January–February) and D and F (March–May) in Grade 2

▶ Read a Level C book (from the small-group book list in Table 4-2) following the regular three-day repeated reading process with the group of students. (See Figure 3-1.)

▶ Then select a Level E book (from the transition book list in Table 4-2) to be used with the transition procedures described below.

▶ Then go back to reading a Level C book (from the small-group book list) following the basic three-day repeated reading format with the group.

▶ The next three-day cycle select a Level E book (from the transition book list) to use with the transition procedures.

▶ Continue until all Level C and E books are completed.

▶ Grade 2 Levels D and F: Continue to alternate between Level D books using the three-day repeated reading process and Level F books using the transition process until all Level D books are gone. Then continue with Level F books for the remainder of the year.

When teachers use the books at EIR Levels E and F, the procedures change.

▶ The teacher works with two students at a time. She may not get to all pairs of students in three days.

▶ The teacher does not first read the book to the children. The teacher has the children read the book "cold" and provides the support each child needs. Children can take turns reading.

▶ The writing component can be continued if time permits.

▶ After the children have read with the teacher, the trained coach listens to the children, one at a time. The trained coach reinforces the children's efforts to sound out words and to use context to unlock meanings of unfamiliar words.

▶ Examples of independent activities for exemplar books for the other EIR children are provided on the lesson planners. (See the teaching resource on the DVD for examples.) Also, the other children can reread old stories or read new ones independently or with a partner.

Figure 5-1 Transition to Independent Reading

▶ The teacher works with two students at a time. They may not get to all pairs of students in three days.

▶ The teacher does not read the book to the children first. The teacher has the children read the book "cold" (that is, not having read it before) and provides the support each child needs. Children can take turns reading.

▶ The writing component can be continued if time permits.

▶ After the children have read with the teacher, the trained coach listens to the children, one at a time. The trained coach reinforces the children's efforts to sound out words and to use context to unlock meanings of unfamiliar words.

Steps for Coaching Pairs of Students

The reason for working with only two children at a time is that the children get more practice with independent reading than if they are in a group of six or seven. In a larger group, they would only get to read every sixth or seventh page as opposed to every other page when reading with a partner. It would be wonderful if every child could read one-on-one with the teacher for transition reading. However, I have found that this takes more than three days, and you should still move on to a new story at the end of three days so the children feel challenged instead of bored from working on the same story for too long.

As you coach during transition, it is important to try to use more general prompts first and move to more specific prompts only if needed (general prompts are listed in the next section). The reason for this is that you want to foster independence in the children. You are not really helping them become independent if you suggest a specific strategy to try.

In addition to using more general prompts, it is important to give children enough wait time. Often, if you are patient, you find that children who have been in EIR will be able to figure out unknown words, especially because of the emphasis in EIR on using strategies to attack words.

In the classroom example and video clip on page 80, you see children engaged in transition reading. As you will notice, there is a fair amount of variation in children's reading ability, but it is important to remember that the children started at different places in the fall. What is important is that the second graders are reading second-grade material (and most of them with some fluency) by the end of the school year.

tips

Tips for Teacher Coaching During the Transition Phase

• Ask questions that will help the child become self-reliant and successful in word attack.
• Don't jump in too quickly to remedy a child's disfluent reading. Interruptions interfere with the flow of the reading. However, reading that is too far off base becomes very confusing to the reader. Balance is the key.
• Remind the child to reread from the beginning of a sentence once pausing to work on a word.

General Prompt to Use Before Reading— Transition Phase

▶ What can you do if it's getting really confusing or if a word doesn't seem right?

General Prompts to Use as Students Are Reading During the Transition Phase

▶ What can you do that can help you? (Reread, keep reading and come back, think about what would make sense, and sound out, etc.)

▶ Is there something you read on this page that isn't right? What can you do about it?

▶ Does the word you just read sound right and look right? Are you happy with *soup* (for *stone*)? Why or why not?

▶ Does that make sense? Think of the story. Think of what's happening.

▶ What can you do to make the word easier/shorter? Is there an ending you can cover up? Is there a word part you recognize? Can you break it into two words (if it's a compound word)?

Praise for self-corrections, successful attempts, and unsuccessful attempts (point out a part that is right); success with coaching depends on you.

ſee it iN ActioN

Transition to Independent Reading

Kathy and two students read a story from *Four on the Shore* by Ed Marshall. (1994). Kathy begins, "I'm going to give you a new book that you have never seen before. I want you to use all of the strategies good readers use when you come to a word you don't know. What are these strategies?" Kira and Francisco say, "Sound it out, chunks, miss it." Kathy stops her to get her to clarify. "What do you mean?" Kira says, "Skip it and come back." Kathy says, "What do you have to ask yourself?" She pauses but gets no response so she adds, "Does it make sense?"

Francisco starts to read. He reads *spider* with a short *i* sound. Kathy coaches, "Try another sound for *i*." Francisco comes up with the correct sound for *spider*. When he reads the sentence, *"Your little brother is getting on my nerves,"* Kathy asks, "What do you think that means?" Kira says, "That you are really mad." Kathy elaborates, "You're mad so he must be doing things."

When Kira reads, Kathy reminds Francisco to follow along and be ready to help Kira if she gets stuck on a word. Kira reads *peace* as *pace*. Kathy coaches her to go back to the word, and Kira reads the word correctly this time. Kathy asks her how she figured it out and Kira says that *ea* says /ee/. Kathy asks, "Does it make sense now?" She also asks Kira to reread, "So we know what it says." When Kira reads *"six one the dot"* for *"six on the dot,"* Kathy has Kira reread to self-correct and asks what *"six on the dot"* means. Kira and Francisco say that it means six o'clock.

Additional Strategies for Word-Recognition Instruction

Once students are developing independence as readers, you may need to help them with vowel combinations and you will probably need to help them learn to decode multisyllabic words successfully. Also, you can conduct oral reading analysis to pinpoint decoding strengths and weaknesses of individual children that you can focus on as you coach them during the transition reading. These topics are discussed below.

Advanced Vowel Chart

Once your students are confident using the short vowel chart to help them decode CVC words and CVCE words (e.g., in early fall in most cases), you want to focus on one-syllable words that contain vowel pairs in your Making

Words instruction and your word-recognition coaching instruction. As you focus on vowel pairs, you want to use the advanced vowel chart in which the most common sounds for vowel pairs are presented. When students are tying to decode a word like *show*, have them use the advanced vowel chart to try one sound for *ow* (as in *cow*) and if that doesn't sound right, try the other sound (as in *snow*). See a sample advanced vowel chart in Figure 3-4 on p. 49.

Decoding Multisyllabic Words

In second grade, children who are struggling with reading will likely need explicit instruction in how to attack multisyllabic words they come across as they are reading. Many struggling readers have not developed the ability to look through an entire longer word. Often these words are told to them by another student or the teacher in an effort to keep things moving along during an oral reading activity.

You can work with your EIR students on a strategy for attacking multisyllabic words. It is important to remind the children that this is a strategy they can use when they are reading on their own and come to a long word they don't instantly recognize. This strategy works best if it is used on a word already in students' listening vocabulary, and many of the words struggling readers come across will, in fact, be words in their listening vocabulary.

It really doesn't matter if the children break a word into the exact syllables as found in the dictionary. Instead, they need to know that a *chunk*, or approximate syllable, has one vowel or vowel team per chunk. They need to learn to be flexible with their sounding out of syllables and blending syllables together. They should be given a copy of the advanced vowel chart to help them remember the most common vowel sounds for a particular vowel or vowel team. Consistently remind students that if one sound doesn't work, they should try another.

The children need to be encouraged that their sounding out will get them close to the real word. As they are blending syllables together, they need to be thinking of a word that is close to what they are saying and that would make sense in the story. I often find that children don't rely on context enough as they are sounding out multisyllabic words. Steps of this strategy for students to use to decode multisyllabic words are:

1. Break the word into chunks (approximate syllables) with one vowel (or vowel team) per chunk.

2. Be flexible as you sound out the chunks, especially with the vowel sounds. That is, if one sound doesn't work, try another.

3. Remember to use context clues.

4. After you sound out the chunks, try it again only faster.

5. Remember that this will only get you close to the right word. Keep thinking of context.

Oral Reading Analysis and Instruction

Once students can read independently at a primer to end of grade one level (EIR Level E), use oral reading analysis (Taylor et al. 1995) with them. This can be done during an oral reading check. In oral reading analysis, you take three 100-word samples of a student's reading of material at their instructional level (92 percent to 97 percent accuracy in word recognition). You analyze these samples to determine one problem area to focus on and then provide instruction in this focus area. As a student does subsequent oral readings, you continue to assess in this focus area, monitoring with a progress chart to document the student's growth in the target area. Once a student has made good progress in one problem area, move to another as needed. The procedures for oral reading analysis are described in Figure 5-2 and a chart you can use to take notes when you conduct oral reading analysis is in Figure 5-3. Potential problem areas and recommendations for instruction follow.

Recording Errors for Oral Reading Analysis

The following is an example of a child's reading of a story and the way the errors would be recorded. (The words that are bolded are the actual text and the errors the child makes that are in parentheses.) A self-correction marked with SC is not counted as an error. SD indicates a child paused on a word but successfully decoded. Note that the child has read this story with 94 percent accuracy, so it is at the appropriate level for oral reading analysis.

> Once upon a time, a man lived in a **hut** (house) with his wife and six children. It was very crowded and **noisy** (nosy) in the hut. So the man went to see the **wise** (wise—SD) man. The wise man told him to put his **chickens** (chicks), goat, and cow in the hut. The man did as he was told. Now it became very, very crowded and **noisy** (noise SC) in the hut. The man was **angry** (any), so he went back to see the wise man. The wise man told him to take the animals out of the hut. The man did as he was told. **Finally** (finally with short *i*), it **did** (does) not seem crowded and noisy in the hut **anymore** (anymore—SD), and the man and his family lived **happily** (happy) ever after.

Oral Reading Analysis
Targeting Your Word-Recognition Instruction

Type of Error or Problem	Instruction/Assessment
Analysis. Student doesn't know how to break a long word into chunks and blend those chunks together.	This is the word-recognition problem that is hardest to correct. Continue to model for a student how to analyze all the letters in a word. Continue to model how to break a word into chunks, using the decoding multisyllabic words strategy discussed in earlier in the chapter. Also, continue to coach a student to use the decoding multisyllabic words strategy himself to figure out hard words.
Automatic. Student makes many errors automatically; that is, the word comes out almost instantly, but it is the wrong word.	At the end of a page, ask the student if he knows what word he read very quickly but read incorrectly. If he does not know, reread the sentence they way he read it, as he reads along, and ask again. Typically, when a student sees what he is doing, he begins to read more carefully and makes fewer automatic errors.
Meaning. Student makes many errors that don't make sense.	At the end of a page, ask the student to identify which word in the sentence didn't make sense as the student read it. If the student doesn't know, reread it for him as he read it. Have him try to figure out the correct word, paying particular attention to the meaning of the text. Typically, once this problem is brought to the student's attention, the number of errors self-corrected goes up quite readily.
Basic sight word. Student makes many errors with basic sight words. (Often these are also automatic errors.)	Often a student doesn't believe he is doing this since he knows the words in isolation. Reread the sentence where the basic sight word was read incorrectly, and ask the child to tell you what word was incorrect. Talk about the importance of not reading so quickly that careless errors are avoided. Again, once the student sees what he is doing, he is usually able to fairly readily correct this problem.
Phonics: symbol sound correspondence. Student makes consistent phonics errors in which he gives the wrong sound for a symbol.	Coach the student, with the use of the short or advanced vowel chart, as he corrects errors of this type.
Omission. Student skips over many or most hard words.	Often, the student doesn't know how to attack multisyllabic words. Model and coach on how to decode a word completely, and praise the child when he does not skip over words.

continues

Figure 5-2 *Oral Reading Analysis*

Oral Reading Analysis, *continued*

Completed Recording Chart

1 Error (or SC/SD word)	2 Analysis Difficulty	3 Automatic Error	4 Meaning Error	5 Other Errors (basic sight words, phonic elements, omissions)	6 Notes
hut (house)		X			
noisy (nosy)		X	X	gave long *o* for *oi*	Teacher told the child the word to get him back on track.
wise (SD)					
chickens (chicks)		X			
noisy (noise—SC)					
angry (any)	X		X		
finally (finally with short *i*)			X	Gave short *i* instead of long *i*.	
did (does)		X		Basic sight word error—gave *does* but word was *did*	
anymore (SD)					Student has a long pause and then comes up with the word
happily (happy)		X			

Key to Columns in Chart

1 **Error or SC/SD Word.** Error due to the substitution of a real word or nonword for the actual word. Substitution is written in parentheses. If a word is omitted, count it as an error and draw a circle around it. (*SC* is used to indicate a self-correction. *SD* is used to indicate a word the student had to stop on to decode, but the student was successful in coming up with the word without even making a self-correction. SC and SD words are not counted as errors.)

2 **Analysis Difficulty.** The student does not seem to be able to work through the entire word but is only able to decode part of it. Error is marked with X in column 2.

3 **Automatic Error.** The student quickly reads the word so that it comes out automatically. However, the word is not read correctly. Error is marked with an X in column 3.

4 **Meaning Error.** The student comes up with a real word or nonword that really doesn't make sense in the context of the text being read. Error is marked with an X in column 4. Be somewhat liberal here. For example, I would not count *house* for *hut, chicks* for *chickens,* or *happy* for *happily* as meaning is seriously impaired. (However, this involves personal judgment and I realize that some would want to count *house* for *hut* as a meaning error. I just tell people to try to be consistent in how they score errors.)

5 **Other Errors.** Typically, these are errors in which the student gave the wrong sound for the symbol (phonic element error), gave the wrong word for a basic sight word (basic sight word error or omitted a word).

6 **Notes.** Here is a place to make comments about the students' reading.

Figure 5-2 Oral Reading Analysis, continued

Comments on Errors

Hut (house)	The child instantly came out with *house* and didn't self-correct.
Noisy (nosy)	The child instantly come out with *nosy*, but it clearly doesn't make sense in the story. Note that this error is counted as both an automatic error and an error that doesn't make sense.
Wise	The child paused on this word because he didn't instantly recognize it. However, when he did say something for the word, it was the correct word. This is not counted as an error.
Chickens (chicks)	The child instantly came out with *chicks* and didn't self-correct.
Noisy (noise–SC)	This time the child reads *noise* for *noisy* but then self-corrects. This is not counted as an error.
Angry (any)	The child does not pronounce the middle sound so this is marked as an error involving an analysis difficulty. Also, *any* does not make sense, and the child should have taken a closer look at the word. Notice that this error was marked as both an error involving analysis and meaning.
Finally (finally with short *i*)	The child read the word with the short vowel sound instead of the long. This is marked as a meaning error since the nonword doesn't make sense. Note that the error wasn't marked as an analysis error since all of the sounds in the word are represented. It's just that the sound given for the *i* is the wrong sound. It was also not marked as an automatic error, which indicates that the child did not instantly come out with the wrong pronunciation for the word.
Did (does)	The child automatically came out with *does* for *did*. Since *did* is a basic sight word, this is noted under column 5.
Anymore–SD	The child paused on this word because he didn't instantly recognize it. However, when he did say something for the word, it was the correct word. This is not counted as an error.
Happily (happy)	The child instantly came out with *happy* and didn't self-correct. It was not marked as an analysis error because the child didn't even take time to analyze it, but automatically came out with the wrong word.
Focus for Instruction	First, it would be best to look across three samples before making a decision about where to focus instruction. Also, this is a personal decision. There is no right answer about where to focus first. However, because five of the child's seven errors were automatic errors, I would be inclined to begin with this first. See p. 83 earlier in the chapter for suggestions pertaining to instruction for this focus. Once a child's progress chart shows improvement in this area, I would focus on and chart progress in correcting errors that didn't make sense.

Figure 5-2 Oral Reading Analysis, continued

Oral Reading Analysis Recording Sheet

1 Error (or SC/SD word)	2 Analysis Difficulty	3 Automatic Error	4 Meaning Error	5 Other Errors (basic sight words, phonic elements, omissions)	6 Notes

Figure 5-3 Oral Reading Analysis Recording Sheet

Summary of Transition Phase

The transition phase is an exciting and challenging time for young readers. While their reading skills are improving and their independence is growing, it is important to continue to support and scaffold their growth, since with this added independence students can sometimes become frustrated. The continued coaching, working with word-recognition strategies, and the conducting and analysis of students' oral reading will enable you to continue the needed support these budding readers need.

Now that you have an idea about the basic three-day routine and the transition phase, we turn to Chapter 6 that presents an accelerated model to be used with some students who progress quickly. Then, Chapter 7 addresses assessment procedures for selecting students for EIR, monitoring progress for students in EIR, and if enough progress is made, having student exit from it.

An Accelerated Model for Some Second Graders

The Accelerated Model is for students who are already reading on an end-of-grade-1 level in the fall of second grade and who, you believe, will need additional reading support in order to be reading on grade level by the end of the school year. I recommend you *begin* these students with books at EIR Level D in October, and use the basic three-day routine for one or two months.

Starting in November or December, these students move from EIR Level D books to the transition procedures with EIR Level F books. By December or January, the teacher moves to the strategies and routines in the Grade 2 EIR Accelerated Model, using books written at a mid- to end-of-second-grade level (see Table 4-1 on page 67 for characteristics of grade 2 books at different EIR levels and Table 4-2 on pages 68–69 for exemplar books for the Accelerated Model). These procedures are similar to the Grade 3 EIR Model (Taylor, *Catching Readers, Grade 3*, 2010), but instead of tutoring a younger student, as in grade 3, grade 2 students coach a partner.

With the accelerated procedures, students continue to receive daily 20-minute group lessons that are *in addition to* their guided reading group. In these intervention lessons, the focus is on the decoding of multisyllabic words, fluency, vocabulary, and comprehension (summarizing and questioning). Many of

the children need this accelerated program in order to develop confidence in decoding multisyllabic words. To help them with this, use the strategy for attacking multisyllabic words described in Chapter 5. Many students in your accelerated EIR group will still need to work on their reading fluency. They can decode with a fair degree of accuracy but they may be very slow. The repeated reading of their EIR story will build their fluency.

For these students, there is also an emphasis on teaching vocabulary, especially at point of contact in the text, engaging students in high-level talk and writing about text, and teaching students comprehension strategies as well as strategies for answering written questions about what they read. A sample three-day routine would look something like Figure 6-1.

Choosing Books and Getting Down to Work

Using Narrative and Informational Texts

Since narrative books tend to be easier to read, in December through February I recommend using more narrative than informational books with the Accelerated Model as children work on their word recognition, fluency, and comprehension of stories. From March through May, I recommend the reverse, using more informational than narrative books so children can work on their comprehension of informational text. As explained next, the comprehension activities for the narrative and informational books are somewhat different.

The children all work on the same book for the three-day lesson. I provide a list of exemplar books for the grade 2 accelerated program in Figure 4-2 in Chapter 4. (On the DVD there are question sheets for the exemplar informational books.)

Word-Recognition Instruction

As your students read part of the book chorally or by taking turns, provide on-the-spot teaching of word-recognition strategies as children get stuck. It is important that you continually remind the others not to call out a word if one child is trying to figure a word out.

The teacher works with the students on the strategy for attacking multisyllabic words (see Chapter 5). Remind the children that this is a strategy they can use when they are reading on their own and come to a long word they don't instantly recognize. This strategy works best if it is used on a word already in students' listening vocabulary, and many of the words struggling readers come across will, in fact, be words in their listening vocabulary. The strategy for decoding multisyllabic words needs to be tied to the use of the advanced vowel chart (also discussed in Chapter 5). I also find it helpful to stress that this strategy will get kids close to the real word. They need to be thinking of a word that will make sense in the story as they are trying to sound out a word. Also, if you have students who are still struggling with word recognition, begin oral reading analysis with them (see Chapter 5).

Three-Day Routine for Grade 2 Accelerated Lessons

DAY 1 LESSON

1. The teacher and students read part of the new book together. They can finish silently.

2. The teacher models and assists in decoding of multisyllabic words as students are reading orally. The meanings of unfamiliar words at point of contact in the story are discussed.

3. The teacher coaches for comprehension on the new EIR book.

4. Time is provided for students to practice reading their new EIR book for fluency. (This could be in the group if time permits or during students' independent work time.)

DAY 2 LESSON

1. The teacher coaches for comprehension on the new EIR book.

2. The teacher and students either summarize and respond to text using the narrative group sheet (for narrative story) or answer written questions (for informational book). If students do not complete the sheet, they can finish it during independent work time on Day 2 or on Day 3. These forms are on the DVD as reproducibles.

3. Children practice reading their book and teacher coaches individual readers, providing help with multisyllabic words in particular.

4. The teacher explains and sends home the individual sheet that prepares students for working with their EIR partner on Day 3.

DAY 3 LESSON

1. The teacher and students discuss strategies for coaching a partner.

2. Partners take turns reading their book to one another.

3. Partners discuss with one another what they wrote on the comprehension and vocabulary sections from their individual take-home sheet.

4. Teacher and students talk about their questions and vocabulary on their take-home sheets. They also discuss how coaching partners went and how to improve it for next time.

5. If they have not already done so and if time allows, students complete their summary on their narrative group sheet or their written answers to questions for their informational book. Alternately, they can complete this during independent work time.

Figure 6-1 Three-Day Routine for Grade 2 Accelerated Lessons

Fluency Instruction

As children practice reading the narrative or informational book they will read on Day 3 with a partner, they are working on their fluency. Because they want to do a good job reading to their partner, they have a reason to take their practicing seriously.

Vocabulary Instruction

Beck, McKeown, and Kucan (2002) discuss the importance of talking about word meanings at point of contact in a story. As students come to words not in their listening vocabulary as they are reading their EIR book, you should stop to talk about these words. As much as possible, ask the children to try to give an approximate meaning for a word by using context clues in the text. Part of the discussion should focus on what clues were used to try to figure out a word's meaning. However, it is important to realize that using context clues is not an easy task for students, and the probability of students learning word meanings from context increases with additional occurrences of the word (Graves 2007).

Coaching for Comprehension (Days 1 and 2)

High-level talk about the text and coaching for comprehension should be brief on Days 1 and 2 (no more than three or four minutes) because children will also be sharing ideas about the story on the group sheet that focuses on narrative or informational text on Day 2 and on the take-home sheet on Day 3. Typically, ask one high-level question about the story for the group to discuss on Day 1 and again on Day 2.

Comprehension of Narrative Text: Summarizing a Story (Day 2)

When you introduce the strategy of summarizing a story, tell students that this is something they will need to do when they are telling their parents or a friend about a book or story they have read. The person they are talking to won't need to hear every detail about the story, so they need to be able to tell about the main ideas in just a few sentences so you pique their interest, but don't give the whole story away. For example, you could say to students, "If you were telling a friend or parent about a book, how could you tell them the most important ideas about the story in just a few sentences so they wouldn't lose interest in what you were telling them?"

Also, discuss with the students that the purpose of summarizing stories is to help readers better understand and remember them. Define summarizing of a story as stating important ideas that tell what happens at the beginning (character, setting, and introduction of a problem), the middle (further development related to the problem), and the end (resolution of the problem and author's message) of a story. Use all of these terms, as modeled on the next page, as you discuss the story with children so they become part of their vocabulary.

Model It

To model summarizing, you might begin by saying, "First, I will give a sentence about the beginning of the story that tells about the characters, setting, and problem." Give a summary sentence from the story in your own words. Talk aloud as you give the reason you came up with this sentence. Then continue by saying, "Next, I will give a sentence about the middle of the story. I'll talk about the development of the problem." Give your sentence for the middle of the story. Talk aloud as you give reasons you came up with this sentence. "Finally, I will give a sentence about the end of the story that tells how the problem got solved. I'll also come up with a sentence that gives what I think is the author's message." Again, talking aloud, give reasons you came up with these two sentences. Continue modeling until the children become familiar with the process.

In addition to modeling, coach students as they try to summarize a story themselves. Ask the children to give one idea that tells about the beginning of the story and includes the main character, the setting, and the character's problem. A sentence such as "If you were to tell a friend about the first part of the story, but you didn't want to tell your friend everything that happened, what would be the most important idea you would say?" could get the discussion started. Get ideas from one or two children and write them on chart paper. Discuss which sentence(s) give a summary idea without too much detail. If no sentence does, discuss ideas with children for taking out the details and coming up with a summary sentence of the main idea instead. If necessary, model a sentence that could work. In the same manner, come up with a summary sentence for the middle and end of the story. In Chapter 2, Diane Swanson provided a good example of coaching her students as they summarized a story.

Write Together

Summarizing is a difficult skill, so early in the year, there may only be time to create a good summary sentence together for just one part of the story. You could suggest sentences for the other parts of the story and tell the students why you generated the sentences you did. At first, vary this routine in subsequent stories by having the children give a summary sentence for the middle of the story while you give beginning and ending sentences, or by having children give a summary sentence for the ending of the story while you give sentences for the beginning and middle of a story. Even though there may not be time to write all three sentences, be sure you have discussed three ideas with them. As children become more proficient, have them give and write all the summary sentences. They should be able to do this by the fourth or fifth story.

Students Write

It is important to keep reminding children why summarizing a story is important to be able to do. Also, as you help children, consistently point out why a sentence makes a good summary sentence and discuss what could be left out or restated if there is too much detail. If there is too much detail in a sentence, ask, "Is that a small part of the story or one of the most important ideas that gets at the character's problem and how he solved it?" and have the child explain the answer.

As soon as students are ready, instead of working on sentences together, discuss possible sentences and let children write their own sentences, using ideas from the discussion. As children become more proficient in summarizing, have them write their own sentences prior to discussion and then have them share with a group. In Figure 6-2, there is a open-ended narrative group sheet that students can use to write story summaries.

Comprehension of Narrative Texts: High-Level Writing (Day 2)

In addition to summarizing a story, the narrative group sheet has students engage in high-level thinking by asking them to identify a part of the story they liked or did not like and to make a personal connection to the story. Also on the narrative group sheet are prompts so that students can focus on vocabulary development by identifying two new words they came across in the story and write their meanings or use them in sentences. They can jot down ideas and

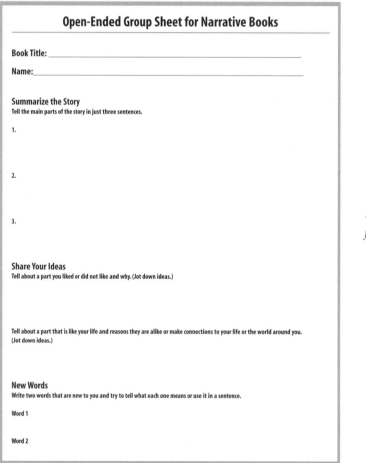

Open-Ended Group Sheet for Narrative Books

Book Title: _____

Name:_____

Summarize the Story
Tell the main parts of the story in just three sentences.

1.

2.

3.

Share Your Ideas
Tell about a part you liked or did not like and why. (Jot down ideas.)

Tell about a part that is like your life and reasons they are alike or make connections to your life or the world around you. (Jot down ideas.)

New Words
Write two words that are new to you and try to tell what each one means or use it in a sentence.

Word 1

Word 2

See the DVD for full-size versions of all the forms in this chapter.

Figure 6-2 Open-Ended Group Sheet for Narrative Stories

share them orally in the group or with a partner. Or you can have them write their ideas in complete sentences.

Comprehension of Informational Texts

When you use informational texts, the focus is on word recognition, fluency, vocabulary, and questioning, just like with narrative texts. However, instead of summarizing a story and completing the open-ended group sheet on a narrative text, students work on writing answers to questions about their informational texts. Writing answers to questions is an activity that students do a lot of in the intermediate grades and above. But it is something that many struggling readers need help with to be successful.

Comprehension: Writing Answers to Questions on an Informational Book (Day 2)

By February or March, you should be starting to use some of the EIR grade 2 accelerated informational books if you haven't already done so. With the informational books, students engage in high-level thinking as they work on answering written questions successfully. Gaetz (1991) found that children have the following problems answering written questions on informational text: (1) They don't read the questions carefully or they don't answer all parts of a question; (2) Their answer is too general; (3) They tell too much detail and never get to the answer; (4) They just have the wrong answer. Children have difficulty summarizing informational text, so teaching strategies for these processes are discussed in this section as well.

Having students answer written questions is important because it helps them read questions correctly, understand the questions, answer all parts of a written question, answer in complete sentences, and get their thoughts down on paper in a clear yet concise manner. As you move toward the more challenging EIR informational books, the questions get more complex in terms of asking the children to summarize the most important ideas or in getting them to explain processes or concepts they have read about. Having these question-answering skills will be valuable to students throughout their school careers.

It goes without saying that another purpose answering questions on the group sheets for informational books is to help students better understand what they have read. Example questions for some of the exemplar grade 2 EIR books are shown in Figure 6-3. Additional question sheets for exemplar grade 2 accelerated books are in Appendix 6-1 on the DVD. The questions tend to get harder as the books get harder (e.g., children are asked to summarize, or give the most important ideas, of a section of a book instead of a page). If you are using your own set of books, you may wish to use the informational question sheets I have prepared as a guide for writing your own. Note how prompts to help students write good, complete answers to questions are in parentheses after some of the questions.

When teaching students about answering questions in writing related to informational books, include the following steps:

▶ Before reading the book, spend a minute or two (but no more) finding out what the children know about the topic. After reading, coach for comprehension with questions such as "What is one new fact you have learned from this book?" or "Could this animal, tree, etc., be found in (our state)? Why or why not? Where?" "How is the place or animal like a place or animal you have seen? Would you like to go to this place? Why or why not?"

▶ Model how to look for answers by saying, "If I were answering this question, first I would think, what does the question ask me to do?" It is important for children to see a variety of ways of finding information to answer the questions.

▶ Model and practice the text look-back strategy: "I will try to remember where I read something that fits with the question and then look back to that part of the book. Often there is a key word in the question that you can search for in the text as a way to look back."

▶ Model using headings. "Sometimes the headings or titles of sections will help me to find the part where the answer is." Model finding headings and title.

Examples of Question Sheets for Informational Books

Animal Parts—Ears by Elizabeth Miles (pages 4–17)

Name: _____

Answer each question with a complete sentence.

1. What is nocturnal? Why does the aardvark have long and pointed ears? Name at least one other nocturnal animal.

2. Which animal ears did you find most interesting? Why? (Be sure to give a reason).

3. Name two animals with rounded ears. Tell how each animal uses it's ears. (Be sure to answer both parts of the q

4. Summarize what you learned about hippopotamus ears in one sentence. (Summarize means to tell the m

Examples of Question Sheets for Informational Books, *continued*

Harry Houdini Escape Artist by Patricia Lakin

Name: _____

Answer each question with a complete sentence.

1. Why do you think Harry Houdini became famous? Name two or three reasons. (Be sure to give enough reasons.)

2. Describe what Harry had to do to become a magician.

3. How did Harry become interested in magic?

4. Summarize pages 23 and 24. (Summarize means to tell the most important ideas. Use your own words).

Figure 6-3 Examples of Question Sheets for Informational Books

▶ Model using pictures. "If the question asks me to describe something, maybe I can use a picture to help me along with information in the text." Show an example of a picture with information in the book.

▶ Model using pictures or charts to make comparisons. "If the question asks me to compare two things maybe I can look at pictures or at a chart." Show an example from the book.

As you read through the questions with the children, be sure they understand what the questions are asking. Coach them with strategies such as the following:

▶ Coach children when they write responses that are too general (e.g., "How are elephant ears different from our ears?" If students say they are large, coach them on how to elaborate on this answer. "How do elephants use their large ears in ways that are different from humans?")

▶ Coach children when their written responses need to be more focused. "How can you say this in fewer words? What are the most important ideas the author wants us to know?"

▶ Coach children when they have the wrong answer. Start by having them look back in the text. Have them reread and ask questions to guide them to a more appropriate response.

  • They may have to put ideas together across two or more sentences because the answer is not explicitly stated in just one sentence (e.g., *Elephants use their ears in different ways. They use them as fans to cool themselves when it is hot.* Question: How do ears help elephants when they are hot?).

  • They may have to use what they already know to help them answer questions (e.g., they might know or be able to make a good guess that a bull elephant holds his ears out to tell smaller elephants to move away. Question: How do small elephant feel when they see a bigger elephant with his ears out?).

At first, children will probably not be able to write all the questions during the EIR lesson, but it is good for them to try to answer all of the questions. This can be done in several ways: Each child writes the response to one question and then shares responses with the group orally; the children answer a number of questions in writing and then do the rest orally; the children work on the questions on Days 2 and 3; or students work on their own or with a partner during independent work time. As the year progresses, however, each child should write answers to all of the questions on their own if possible. Be sure that children can tell you how they got their answers because this is also an important component to monitoring comprehension.

Comprehension Strategy Instruction: Summarizing Informational Text

For some of the written questions, students are asked if they can summarize a section of their informational text. They will need modeling and coaching from you to learn how to do this. First, explain to the students that summarizing an informational text means being able to describe the most important ideas contained in a paragraph, a page, or a section of text. Tell them it is impossible to remember all the ideas in informational text so it is important to learn how to remember and identify the most important ideas. The steps to follow are:

▶ Model how to read one paragraph, page, or section of informational text at a time and select two or three words from the text that reflects its topic (e.g., "This page was about *elephant ears*."). This is an "about statement."

▶ Model (talk aloud) as you turn the topic or "about statement" into a complete sentence or two that reflects the most important ideas. Write the idea(s) on the board. *Elephants use their large ears in ways humans don't. They use them as fans to cool off when it is hot. They use them to communicate with others. This is an "about statement."*

▶ Show students how to make their answers concise. Students have a tendency to write too many ideas until they learn how to limit the number of details. Ask, "What do you think are the most important ideas the author wanted you to remember?"

▶ Coach by talking about why certain ideas would not be good main idea statements because they are too general (*Elephants' ears are big.*) or too specific (*The skin on elephants' ears is more than an inch thick.*), and why others aren't that important (*Their ears are gray*).

In Chapter 2 May Holder and Diane Swanson give good examples of teaching students how to summarize informational text.

Work to Complete at Home: Preparation for Partner Work (Day 2)

In addition to practicing at school, children are to take their books home for additional fluency practice on Day 2. The children will also complete the individual take-home sheet at home. In addition to practicing reading their story, they are to write down two vocabulary words and one question that gets them to think and that they will discuss with their EIR partner on Day 3 (see Figure 6-4 and the DVD).

Working with a Partner (Day 3)

On Day 3, students read their story with a partner. Remind the listeners that they should not tell their partner a word if he or she gets stuck while reading, but give them a hint instead. Review strategies for coaching partners in Chapter 3. Then, partners take turns reading their book to one another. While moving around the groups, coach students on their own coaching or help them figure out difficult words if both children are stuck.

Next, partners discuss with one another the "juicy" questions they wrote on their individual take-home sheets. Encourage students to elaborate on their thinking as they answer these questions. Students also discuss the meanings of the vocabulary words they wrote on their take-home sheets.

Give the group feedback on their comprehension questions, praising them for high-level questions and coaching them on how to turn low-level questions into high-level ones for the future. Individuals share a few of their favorite words from their take-home sheets and the group discusses their meanings. Also discuss how coaching and working with partners went and how to improve for next time. Students complete their story summaries (narrative group sheets) or question sheets (informational books) if there is time and this work is not finished, or they can do this during independent work time.

Independent Take-Home Sheet

Book Title: _____

Name: _____ **Parent Signature:** _____

Reading for Fluency

I practiced my story _____ times.

_____ I am ready to read it to my partner.

_____ I need to practice some more.

Discussion

Write down one question about the story that makes you think and that you and your partner can discuss.

New Words

Write down two words to ask/tell your partner about (what they mean).

Word 1

Word 2

© 2010 by Barbara M. Taylor from *Catching Readers, Grade 2*. Portsmouth, NH: Heinemann.

Figure 6-4 Independent Take-Home Sheet

Assessing Second Graders in EIR

In this chapter, I share the fall assessments that help you determine which of your second graders will benefit from supplemental reading instruction, as well as advice for monitoring their reading progress throughout the year and in the spring.

Fall Assessments

In September, teachers assess second graders to see if there are students who need supplemental instruction in order to catch up to grade-level reading expectations. These assessments are typical of the kinds of classroom-based assessments teachers give all their students at the beginning of the school year. However, to be as certain as you can that the right students are getting supplemental reading help through EIR lessons, use an informal reading inventory (IRI) (e.g. Leslie and Caldwell 2006) with any child you think needs extra support. Directions for administering an informal reading inventory in the fall are provided in Figure 7-1 Also, refer to the summarizing rubric (Figure 7-2) and the fall summary sheet to record scores (Figure 7-3) as you read through the chapter. These figures are all available full-size on the DVD.

Directions for Grade 2 Fall Assessments

Oral reading: Errors include substitutions, omissions, teacher-assisted or teacher-pronounced words. Self-corrections, repetitions, or hesitations are *not* errors.

Step 1. Have student read a primer-level passage from an IRI for 1 minute. Put a check mark above each word read incorrectly (error). If a student gets stuck on a word, wait about five seconds then tell him the word. Mark the last word read in the minute.

Step 2. Continue reading the selection to the end, marking the errors made. Now that you are no longer timing the student, use your own judgment on time before telling a word, but probably wait about 5 seconds. Stop if the child is reading at less than 90 percent accuracy on primer informal reading inventory (IRI) passage, and do not do the summarizing or comprehension questions (continue to Steps 5, 6, and 7).

Step 3. Have student summarize the selection. Use four-point rubric to score (see the Summarizing Rubric, Figure 7–2). Select the rubric score 1, 2, 3, or 4 that best fits the student's summary and record it on the Fall Summary Sheet.

Step 4. Ask student questions for selection. Record the percent of questions correct on the summary sheet.

Step 5. Count the number of words read correctly in one minute. Record on summary sheet.

Step 6. Count the number of errors in total selection. Calculate word recognition accuracy and record on summary sheet.

If a student is reading at 90 percent accuracy or above on a primer passage, continue to grade 1 passage and repeat Steps 1–6. Stop if the child is at less than 90 percent word-recognition accuracy and do not do the summarizing or comprehension questions.

Figure 7-1 Directions for Grade 2 Fall Assessment

Summarizing Rubric for Grades 1–4

Passage _____   Child _____

Summarizing: Tell the most important ideas you just read about.

Record student's response as best as possible:

Score:

Scoring Guide

1	2	3	4
✓ Student offers little or no information about the selection. ✓ Summary is incomprehensible. ✓ Stated ideas do not relate to the selection.	✓ Student relates details only. ✓ Student is unable to recall the gist of the selection. ✓ Summary is incomplete or ideas are misconstrued.	✓ Student relates some main ideas and some supporting details. ✓ Summary is fairly coherent.	✓ All major points and appropriate supporting details are included. ✓ High degree of completeness and coherence ✓ Student generalizes beyond the text.

Figure 7-2 Summarizing Rubric for Grades 1–4

Grade 2 Fall Summary Sheet

Teacher: _____   Date: _____

Grade 2	Primer Passage					Grade 1 Passage				
Student	Words Correct in First Minute	Number of Errors in Total Passage	Word-Recognition Accuracy (Percent Correct)	Summary Score (4-point rubric)	Questions Correct (Percent)	Words Correct in First Minute	Number of Errors in Total Passage	Word-Recognition Accuracy (Percent Correct)	Summary Score (4-point Rubric)	Questions Correct (Percent)

Figure 7-3 Grade 2 Fall Summary Sheet

See the DVD for full-size versions of all the forms in this chapter.

What to Look For

In general, we are first looking for second graders who are not yet reading (e.g., not able to decode a primer-level passage with at least 90 percent accuracy). Other students who are having some difficulty with reading may benefit from the Accelerated Model.

Guidelines to help you decide who would benefit from EIR lessons are:

▶ If a child is unable to read a primer-level passage from an informal reading inventory with 90 percent accuracy and is reading at less than 35 wcpm, the child should be in an EIR group.

▶ If a child is able to read a primer-level passage from an informal reading inventory with 90 percent accuracy but cannot read an end-of-first-grade passage with 90 percent accuracy and is reading at about 35 to 45 wcpm, the child should be in an EIR group if there is room, (i.e., less than seven children in the group.)

▶ If a child can decode a first-grade passage from an informal reading inventory with 92 percent to 97 percent accuracy but she has difficulty with fluency (e.g., reading at about 35 to 45 wcpm) or comprehension (e.g., summary score of 1 or 2 and/or less than 70 percent correct on questions, place the child in a group using the EIR Accelerated Model (see Chapter 6).

Providing for Second Graders Who Have Varying Needs in Reading

Sometimes I am asked if a child who is not yet reading independently in the fall of grade 2 should be placed in grade 1 EIR lessons, and my answer is always, "No, put them in grade 2 EIR lessons so they have a chance of reading on a grade 2 level by the end of the year." The grade 1 EIR model is designed to get a child to a primer or end-of-grade-1 reading level by May.

The grade 2 EIR model was created with the expectation that second graders, including ELLs and students with learning disabilities, can and will get farther than a first-grade reading level by the end of the year. So, instead of the grade 1 EIR books, routines, and strategies, even for those children who seem to be non-readers, the grade 2 EIR model is the way to go. The grade 2 EIR model starts out at the same level as the grade 1 EIR model but it accelerates more quickly.

Grouping Considerations

The following are some grouping considerations that were covered earlier in the book, but they're worth revisiting now:

▶ **Maximum number of students in the groups: seven.** If there are more than seven children in your room in need of EIR, I would recommend splitting the group into two groups. If you have Title 1 at your school, perhaps the Title 1 teacher could take one group and you could take the other. With a situation like this, a number of teachers have reported switching groups periodically so they can monitor the strengths and weaknesses of all of their struggling readers.

▶ **Arrange two groups for optimum student participation.** If you have enough students for two groups, put the faster-progressing students in one group and the students who may need more support in the other. This way the more-advanced students won't be calling out answers while the other students are still thinking. Also, the students who are progressing more slowly will be less inclined to feel discouraged if they do not feel others in their group are catching on more quickly.

▶ **Remember, children can quit attending an EIR if they are making excellent progress in reading.** Some students will catch up to their grade-level peers and therefore not need EIR beyond, say, February, or sometimes even sooner. Guidelines to help you decide if a child is ready to be taken out of EIR are provided in this chapter.

▶ **Reserve EIR instruction for teachers only.** Children at risk of reading failure desperately need quality, supplemental reading instruction from a certified teacher. Instructional aides don't have sufficient background.

▶ **ELLs do well in EIR.** Often, the questions come up as to whether or how to place ELL students in EIR. If they do poorly on the fall assessment, I would put them in an EIR group in the fall unless they have the opportunity to learn to read in their first language. You do not want to take the chance of preventing any student from learning to read by postponing their participation in EIR to after the first of the year.

▶ **Special education students do well in EIR.** I have found EIR also works well with students who have learning disabilities. No modifications to the program are recommended. Developmentally and cognitively delayed students also learn well in the EIR program, but more predictable books have been found to be useful to keep the children feeling successful. I would start out with the regular books and switch to more predictable titles by Levels B or C, if needed, as the regular EIR stories get harder and less predictable.

▶ **The earlier the better!** Sometimes teachers ask me if they should wait to put a child in EIR since he or she scored so low on all the assessments. My response is always, "No, put them in EIR in the fall." If you wait to put your lowest students in EIR in January, for example, it is very likely they won't catch up to their grade-level peers by May.

Assessing Students' Progress in Reading During the School Year

It is always important to continually assess students' development as readers; therefore, embedded within the EIR model are opportunities for teachers to monitor and document students' progress. Conducting oral reading checks, assessing word-recognition fluency, and conducting oral reading analysis (see Chapter 5) are three assessment measures recommended when implementing EIR.

Conducting Oral Reading Checks

Regular monitoring of progress is an important part of EIR. Oral reading checks are used to measure who is making good progress in the program. An oral reading check should be done with every child about every other story on average during Step 1 of Days, 1, 2, and/or 3 of the EIR routine. The oral reading check should be taken on the story just finished within a few days or so after the child moves on to a new story.

In EIR, the oral reading check is used first and foremost to monitor children's progress rather than to do an analysis of errors. In second grade, children reading "old" (familiar) EIR stories with at least 90 percent accuracy are making good progress.

During an oral reading check, tell the child that you won't be coaching as much as you usually do because you want to see what the child can do on her own. If a child is getting mixed up, you can coach (or tell a child a word if it is a hard word), but try to do this sparingly for the oral reading check. If a child is frustrated, you can stop. However, you should try to get the child to read through the story if possible.

To take an oral reading check, you can simply make check marks on a sheet of paper for words read correctly. For words read incorrectly, write the word the child actually says. If the child self-corrects, mark this with "SC" next to the word read incorrectly that you wrote down. If you end up telling the child a word, mark this with a "TH" for teacher help.

Count errors, including words you did have to tell the child, but do not include repetitions or self-corrections in this count. Out of the total number of words read, subtract the number of errors to determine the total number of words read correctly. Divide the number of words read correctly out of the number of words read to get the word-recognition accuracy score (see an example in Figure 7-4).

At first, children in second grade may not do as well as hoped for on their oral reading check, but after a few checks, they should move above the 90 percent accuracy mark. If a child is consistently falling below 90 percent accuracy on his oral reading check, he needs more individual help. Perhaps this is a child you attend to more often during the time you coach individuals. Perhaps this is a child who works more than once a day with a one-on-one coach. This may also be a child who would benefit from one-on-one tutoring if that is available at your school. An example of an oral reading check is in Figure 7-4. An oral reading check summary sheet is in Figure 7-5.

Based on my research, I have found that children who are in lessons following in the basic EIR model and who are able to read their story with at least 90 percent accuracy after spending three to four days on it are making good progress in the program (Taylor et al. 1992). (Their percentage may be lower on the first few stories, but it should be above the 90 percent accuracy level after this.) More specifically, students who come to second grade not yet reading but who are consistently above 90 percent accuracy on their oral

Example of an Oral Reading Check

Shown here is an oral reading check for the sample reading below. The words in parentheses in the passage are what the child read incorrectly. The TH that follows a word is used to indicate that the teacher told the child the word (teacher help). The SC that follows a word is used to indicate that the child self-corrected an error. SD indicates that the child paused on the word but successfully decoded it.

The Farmer and the Noisy Hut

Once upon a time, a man lived in a **hut (house)** with his wife and six children.

It was very crowded (TH) and **noisy (nosy)** in the hut.

So the man went to see the **wise (wise—SD)** man.

The wise man told him to put his **chickens (chicks)**, goat, and cow in the hut.

The man did as he was told.

Now it became very, very crowded and **noisy (noise SC)** in the hut.

The man was **angry (any)**, so he went back to see the wise man.

The wise man told him to take the animals out of the hut.

The man did as he was told.

Finally (finally with short i), it **did (does)** not seem crowded and noisy in the hut anymore **(anymore—long pause, SD)**,

and the man and his family lived **happily (happy)** ever after.

✓ ✓ ✓ ✓ ✓ ✓ ✓ ✓ house ✓ ✓ ✓ ✓ ✓
✓ ✓ ✓ ✓ ✓ nosy ✓ ✓ ✓
✓ ✓ ✓ ✓ ✓ ✓ ✓ ✓ ✓
✓ ✓ ✓ ✓ ✓ ✓ ✓ chicks ✓ ✓ ✓ ✓ ✓ ✓

✓ ✓ ✓ ✓ ✓ ✓
✓ ✓ ✓ ✓ ✓ ✓ ✓ noise(SC) ✓ ✓ ✓

✓ ✓ ✓ any ✓ ✓ ✓ ✓ ✓ ✓ ✓ ✓
✓ ✓ ✓ ✓ ✓ ✓ ✓ ✓ ✓ ✓ ✓ ✓
✓ ✓ ✓ ✓ ✓ ✓ ✓

Finally (short i) ✓ does ✓ ✓ ✓ ✓ ✓ ✓ ✓ ✓ anymore (SD)

✓ ✓ ✓ ✓ ✓ ✓ happy ✓ ✓

115 words correct/122 words = 94 percent word recognition accuracy

Figure 7-4 Example of an Oral Reading Check

Oral Reading Check Summary Sheet

Student	Level		Level		Level		Level	
	Story		Story		Story		Story	
	Score (%)	Date Given	Score (%)	Date Given	Score (%)	Date Given	Score (%)	Date Given

Figure 7-5 Oral Reading Check Summary Sheet

reading check typically are reading books, sight unseen, at a mid-second-grade level or better by May.

Assessing Word-Recognition Fluency

Skilled readers are fluent readers. They are able to read orally with accuracy, automaticity, speed, proper phrasing, and expression. The benefit of fluent reading is that the reader can devote maximum cognitive capacity to the meaning of text (Kuhn and Stahl 2003; NRP 2000). Less fluent readers focus attention on decoding individual words and tend to read in a choppy, word-by-word manner.

One good measure of fluent reading for students reading on a first-to-third-grade level is the number of words read correctly on a grade-level passage in one minute. The number of words read correctly in a minute has been found to be a useful indicator of a student's reading ability (Fuchs et al. 2001).

Hasbrouck and Tindal (2006) published fall, winter, and spring oral reading norms expressed in wcpm (words correct per minute) for more than 15,000 students in first through fifth grades. The mean scores and standard deviations are presented in Table 7-1.

Mean Words Correct Per Minute Scores and Standard Deviations

Grade	Mean Fall Score	Mean Winter Score	Mean Spring Score
1		23 (32)	53 (39)
2	51 (37)	72 (41)	89 (42)
3	71 (40)	92 (43)	107 (44)
4	94 (40)	112 (41)	123 (43)
5	110 (45)	127 (44)	139 (45)

Note: Standard deviations appear in parentheses.

Adapted from Hasbrouck and Tindal (2006).

Table 7-1 Mean Words Correct Per Minute Scores and Standard Deviations

In addition to assessing students' reading fluency through a wcpm score, rubrics have been developed to assess student phrasing and expression while reading. An oral reading fluency scale, developed by the National Assessment of Educational Practice (NAEP), is presented in Figure 7-6.

NAEP's Oral Reading Fluency Scale

Level 4   Reads primarily in larger, meaningful phrase groups. Although some regressions, repetitions, and deviations from text may be present, these do not appear to detract from the overall structure of the story. Preservation of the author's syntax is consistent. Some or most of the story is read with expressive interpretation.

Level 3   Reads primarily in three- or four-word phrase groups. Some smaller groupings may be present. However, the majority of phrasing seems appropriate and preserves the syntax of the author. Little or no expressive interpretation is present.

Level 2   Reads primarily in two-word phrases with some three- or four-word groupings. Some word-by-word reading may be present. Word groupings may seem awkward and unrelated to larger context of sentence or passage.

Level 1   Reads primarily word by word. Occasional two-word or three-word phrases may occur but these are infrequent and/or they do not preserve meaningful syntax.

From http://nces.ed.gov/pubs95/web/95762.asp, U.S. Department of Education, National Center for Education Statistics

Figure 7-6 NAEP's Oral Reading Fluency Scale

Taking Children Out of EIR

There will be some children who won't need EIR after the first of the year, but I have not found this to be too common. In general, however, I recommend that you be conservative and not discontinue a child too quickly. The follow guidelines can help you determine whether a child should quit attending EIR lessons.

Criteria for Removing a Child from EIR

▶ The child is able to read the new book or books of the week with 99 percent to 100 percent accuracy at least three weeks in a row on an oral reading check.

▶ The child has had EIR lessons for at least three months.

▶ When working in a group, the child is clearly ahead of other children.

▶ The child's performance in the classroom reading program shows that he or she is performing effectively in grade-level texts. The child would have to be able to read grade-level texts with at least 92 percent to 100 percent accuracy. (To assess, do an oral reading check on the next story the child will be reading from the school's reading series. This story should be read cold; that is, the child has not read or had an adult read it to him or her.)

▶ The child is reading close to 90 words correct per minute.

Watch closely to see if children you have released are making good progress in the regular program. If not, they may need to rejoin the EIR group.

Spring Assessments

Use an informal reading inventory to assess the reading progress of children who have been in the grade 2 EIR program. Directions for administering portions of this test are provided in Figure 7-7. For a summary sheet to record scores in, see Figure 7-8. These forms are available full-size on the DVD.

First, you should be looking for children's ability to decode a second-grade level passage with at least 92 percent accuracy. Our hope is that our second graders, including ELLs and students with learning disabilities, get to an end-of-grade-2 reading level by the end of the year. Over the years, I have found, on average, that 85 percent of the children in the grade 2 EIR program, who enter second grade reading at a primer level or lower, are reading on a grade 2 level by May (Taylor 2001).

Second, you should be looking at a child's fluency as measured by words correct per minute. In a national study, Taylor et al. (2000) found that the average second-grade student on an informal reading inventory was able to read the grade 2 passage in May with 89 words correct per minute. Hasbrouck and Tindal (2006) also found that the average fluency score for second graders at the end of the year was 89 words correct per minute.

Third, you need to consider a child's comprehension as measured by answering passage questions and summarizing the passage. The child should

Directions for Grade 2 Spring Assessment

Oral reading: Errors include substitutions, omissions, teacher-assisted or teacher-pronounced words. Self-corrections, repetitions, or hesitations are *not* errors.

Step 1. Have student read an end-of-grade-2 passage from an IRI for one minute. Put a check mark above each word read incorrectly (error). If a student gets stuck on a word wait about 5 seconds then tell the student the word. Mark the last word read in the minute.

Step 2. Continue reading the passage to the end, marking the errors made. Now that you are no longer timing the student, use your own judgment on time before telling a word, but probably wait about 5 seconds. Stop if the child falls below 90 percent accuracy in word recognition on the grade 2 passage. Do not do the summarizing or comprehension questions (continue to Steps 5 and 6).

Step 3. Have student summarize the story. Use 4-point rubric to score. Record score 1, 2, 3, or 4 on summary sheet.

Step 4. Ask student questions for passage. Record the percent of questions correct on the summary sheet.

Step 5. Count the number of words read correctly in one minute. Record on summary sheet.

Step 6. Count the number of errors in total passage. Calculate word recognition accuracy and record on summary sheet.

If you need to move down to a grade 1 passage (because the child read the grade 2 passage with less than 90 percent accuracy), or can continue on to a grade 3 passage (because the child read the grade 2 passage with 90 percent accuracy or better), repeat Steps 1–6 and record in second table on summary sheet.

Figure 7-7 Directions for Grade 2 Spring Assessment

Grade 2 Spring Summary Sheet

Grade 2	Grade 2 Passage				Grade 1 or Grade 3 Level Passage			
Student	Words Correct in First Minute	Word-Reconition Accuracy (% Correct)	Summarizing Score (4-Point Runric)	Questions Correct (%)	Words Correct in First Minute	Word-Recognition Accuracy (% Correct)	Summarizing Score (4-Point Rubric)	Questions Correct (%)

Figure 7-8 Grade 2 Spring Summary Sheet

be able to answer at least 70 percent of the questions correctly and get a summarizing score of 3 or 4 (as detailed earlier in the rubric). According to the same national study mentioned above, the average second-grade reader had a summarizing score of 3.2 (Taylor et al. 2000).

Children falling below 90 percent accuracy on grade 2 passages in the spring will probably need supplemental help in word recognition in the fall of third grade. Children falling below 70 wcpm at the end of grade 2 may need to work on fluency in the fall of third grade. Children who can tell little about the grade 2 passages (summarizing score of 1 or 2) or are at the frustration level on the questions (falling below 70 percent correct) may need to work on comprehension in the fall. (See Taylor 2010c.)

Summary of Assessment Procedures

In this chapter we have looked at assessment procedures that will help you identify students who will benefit from EIR lessons. We have also talked about ongoing assessment techniques that will help you evaluate students' reading progress during the year. We also covered end-of-year assessment procedures that will help you determine students' reading progress and abilities. This progress make the extra effort required to provide EIR lessons seem very worthwhile.

Managing Your Reading Block with EIR

chapter

8

I n this chapter, we look at how the EIR lessons fit within the reading block, reading/writing block, or literacy block. Teachers arrange their literacy time in ways that suit their individual teaching styles and students' needs, and the EIR lessons are effective in many different iterations of effective instruction. However, as discussed briefly in Chapter 1, some components need to be in place no matter what: whole-group instruction, small-group instruction (including guided reading and EIR lessons), and independent reading/independent work time for students for when the teacher is with small groups.

Take a look at your reading block schedule. Research indicates that effective teachers balance whole-class and small-group instruction (Pressley et al. 2003; Taylor et al. 2007). My research shows that too much time on whole-group instruction (e.g., 60 percent of the time or more) or small group (e.g., 85 percent of the time or more) is negatively related to students' reading growth (Taylor et al. 2003; 2007).

Keeping balance in mind, you may find it is most powerful to begin the reading block with a whole-group lesson in which you provide explicit instruction in a reading skill or strategy, using a high-quality trade book or literature from a basal reader anthology. You teach the reading skill in the context of engaging with and enjoying a story or piece of nonfiction. Then you move into small, guided reading groups to differentiate instruction, including follow-up instruction on the skill or strategy covered in the whole-group lesson. You and your students should be aware of the connection between whole-group, small-group, and one-on-one instruction; it should not be a hidden thread but a visible thread. Students are in a much better position to learn when you explicitly name the connection you want them to make. For example, in a whole-class group, the teacher might read a story and focus on the big idea. Students would work again on a story's big idea in small groups and on their own, thus identifying the big idea of a story in all three instructional settings. Or, a teacher might directly name the shared purpose of multiple activities on the same day: "As you read on your own, I want you to practice summarizing, just as we did during our whole-group lesson."

Helpful Resources

Fountas, I. C. , and G. S. Pinnell. 1996. *Guided Reading: Good First Teaching for All Children.* Portsmouth, NH: Heinemann.

Lapp, D., D. Fisher, and T. D. Wolsey. 2009. *Literacy Growth for Every Child: Differentiated Small-Group Instruction, K–6.* New York: Guilford.

Manning, M., G. Morrison, and D. Camp. 2009. *Creating the Best Literacy Block Ever.* New York: Scholastic.

Pressley, M. 2006. *Reading Instruction That Works: The Case for Balanced Teaching.* 3rd ed. New York: Guilford.

Routman, R. 2008. *Teaching Essentials.* Portsmouth, NH: Heinemann.

———. 2003. *Reading Essentials.* Portsmouth, NH: Heinemann

Serravallo, J. 2010. *Teaching Reading in Small Groups.* Portsmouth, NH: Heinemann.

Southall, M. 2009. *Differentiated Small-Group Reading Lessons.* New York: Scholastic.

Taberski, S. 2000. *On Solid Ground: Strategies for Teaching Reading K–3.* Portsmouth, NH: Heinemann.

Tyner, B. 2009. *Small-Group Reading Instruction: A Differentiated Teaching Model for Beginning and Struggling Readers.* Newark, DE: International Reading Association.

Tyner, B., and S. E. Green. 2005. *Small-Group Reading Instruction: A Differentiated Teaching Model for Intermediate Readers, Grades 3–8.* Newark, DE: International Reading Association.

Walpole, S., and M. C. McKenna. 2009. *How to Plan Differentiated Reading Instruction: Resources for Grades K–3.* New York: Guilford.

Effective teachers use good classroom management practices (Pressley et al. 2003). There are many excellent professional books, such as those listed in the previous box, that can help you develop and manage a dynamic literacy block, but for now, here are a few key components:

▶ Work with students to establish classroom rules and routines to minimize disruptions and to provide for smooth transitions within and between lessons.

▶ Use positive language and a motivating, engaging environment to impact students' behavior.

▶ Make a conscious effort to develop self-regulated, independent learners.

▶ Create a positive classroom atmosphere by demonstrating enthusiasm for learning, and have high expectations for your students.

Management Ideas

Some of the primary-grade teachers I have worked with have engaged in the following practices to promote a constructive, classroom environment. Notice that teachers negotiate the criteria for behavior with students and refine it through the year. Some teachers generate and revise lists of expected behaviors and routines as a shared writing activity. Techniques to promote positive classroom environments include the following:

How to Promote Positive Classroom Environments

▶ Generate rules as a class during the first week of school.

▶ Read through classroom rules with students and talk about them at the morning meeting.

▶ Ask students to evaluate their actions after a discussion or activity, focusing on strengths and areas in need of improvement.

▶ Teach students how to compliment each other and encourage them to be respectful of one another.

▶ Have a brief class meeting at the end of the day and ask students how they thought their behaviors were that day, based on the rules they had generated as a class.

▶ Use routines and procedures to handle disruptions effectively and efficiently.

▶ Use routines and procedures to provide for smooth transitions within and between lessons.

▶ Show students that you care about them as individuals, but also let them know that you will be firm, holding them to high standards as learners and good citizens.

▶ Give specific, constructive feedback to students regularly, provide encouragement, and challenge them to think more deeply.

▶ Offer sincere praise to students, as a group or one-on-one, when they have demonstrated behaviors reflected in your classroom rules as well as in school goals defining the school community, often displayed when you enter a building.

Reading Block Schedules: Examples of Effective Balance

May Holder, Leah Davis, and Diane Swanson, the three teachers you met in Chapters 1 and 2, typically start their reading block with a 20- to 30-minute whole-group lesson (often broken up with brief partner work) and then move into a 20-minute small-group lessons in which they provide differentiated instruction depending on students' reading abilities and needs. All three teachers also provide EIR lessons to their less able readers. They explicitly state their lesson purposes in both whole- and small-group lessons. They move at an efficient pace, guided by lesson goals, and typically meet with all of their guided groups every day. In the sections that follow, each of the teacher's schedules is presented and a brief discussion of how the reading block might unfold is provided.

All three teachers provide challenging learning activities, including activities for independent work time. They have students engage in independent and partner work related to high-level talk and writing in response to what they are reading, student-led discussions of book club texts, researching and writing reports based on books of their choosing, and independent reading for pleasure from books of their own choosing. In second grade, students should read for about 30 minutes a day for pleasure (Taylor et al. 2000). This will build their fluency and their motivation to read and will also enhance their reading abilities.

May Holder's Daily Reading Block Schedule

May has a 100-minute reading block in the morning. She spends about 30 minutes a day on a whole-group lesson and about 70 minutes a day on four guided reading groups. After lunch, she works with one EIR group for 20 minutes (which is a second shot of quality instruction for her struggling readers). During this time, average and above-average readers continue with their independent work from the morning.

Average and above-average readers spend about 70 minutes a day and below-average readers spend about 50 minutes a day on independent learning activities. May has a parent, senior citizen, or student from a nearby community college in her classroom during her morning reading block. This volunteer listens to EIR students reread their EIR stories and provides assistance as students are engaged in independent work activities.

May's average and above-average readers typically have three different activities to work on during their independent work time that follow-up on learning objectives from their whole- or small-group lesson. The follow-up activities involve reading, rereading, writing, and discussing text related to their earlier lesson. They also spend about 30 minutes a day doing independent reading. They engage in pleasure reading from books of their own choosing, reading for a book club, or reading to learn new information. They may also have a book club discussion during this time.

Typically, the below-average readers engage in two independent activities that follow-up the whole-group, small-group, or EIR lessons. They also spend about 30 minutes a day in independent reading. How might you adapt May's schedule for your classroom?

May's Daily Groups

9:00–9:30	Whole-Group Lesson	10:05–10:25	Small-Group 3
9:30–9:50	Small-Group 1	10:25–10:40	Small-Group 4
9:50–10:05	Small-Group 2	12:00–12:20	EIR Lesson

May's Typical Daily Reading Block at a Glance

Whole-Group Lesson (30 minutes)	Small-Group Lesson (15–20 min. for each group using leveled texts)	EIR Lesson (20 minutes)	Group	Activities for Independent Work Time
Read basal reader selection, target comprehension strategy, teach vocabulary at point of contact, discuss high-level questions, review activities for work time	Teach phonics as needed, read text and coach in word-recognition strategies, discuss vocabulary at point of contact, provide follow-up to comprehension strategy taught in whole group, discuss high-level questions about leveled text			
X	X		Above-Average Readers* (Group 1)	*Activity 1:* Reading or rereading, writing, discussing as follow-up to whole-group text
				Activity 2: Reading or rereading, writing, discussing as follow-up to small-group text
				Activity 3: Reading or rereading, writing, discussing text unrelated to whole- or small-group lesson
				Activity 4: Reading for pleasure from book of choice
X	X		Average Readers* (Groups 2 and 3)	Activity 1
				Activity 2
				Activity 3
				Activity 4
X	X		Below-Average Readers** (Group 4)	Activity 1
		X		Activity 2 or 3
				Activity 4

*10–20 minutes for each activity for a total of 60 minutes

**10–20 minutes for each activity for a total of 40 minutes

Independent Activities in May Holder's Classroom

Activities that May structures for her students include working independently, with a partner, or in a small group on reading, rereading for fluency, writing in a journal, writing on an open response sheet, talking with others about what they have read or written about in their reading, and using the computer to read or gather new information. Examples, some of which we read about in Chapter 2, include the following:

▶ **Complete strategy work as a follow-up to small-group lesson:**

- Finish writing the middle and end of a story summary that was started in their guided reading group.

- Read and summarize book at the just-right reading level on inventors, polar bears, or walruses after practicing summarizing an article about blizzards read in a whole-group lesson.

▶ **Write in reader response journals and share:**

- Respond to high-level questions the teacher has written on the board and write about a chore they do at home.

- Generate questions, write down interesting or unknown words, and formulate summaries in their journals.

▶ **Write on index cards and share:**

- Write in-the-book and in-the-head questions to ask the next day in their small group.

▶ **Write on sticky notes and share:**

- Write down the meanings of unknown words from small-group story; write down words for "Sticky Note Wednesday."

- Write down "dazzling words" to share.

- Jot down ideas or vocabulary that need clarifying from texts read or note phrases to make connections to texts read.

▶ **Read, write, and discuss in book clubs:**

- Read the next chapter and write good discussion questions.

▶ **Read, write, and share ideas from informational books:**

- Complete a summary of a second type of lizard and its adaptations.

- Write about what was interesting of surprising after reading about horned lizards in a whole-group lesson.

- Select a weather topic, do additional reading, and write three interesting facts to share with whole class after reading about blizzards in whole group.

▶ **Engage in independent reading for pleasure at just-right (independent) reading level and keep a log.**

Leah Davis' Daily Reading Block Schedule

Leah has a 110-minute reading block. She begins with a whole-group lesson that lasts for 30 to 45 minutes, depending on the lesson's purpose. She spends from 50 to 60 minutes on three guided reading groups and 20 minutes on one EIR group (which is a second shot of quality instruction for her struggling readers). Average and above-average readers spend from 50 to 60 minutes a day on independent learning activities and below-average readers spend from 30 to 40 minutes a day on independent learning activities. She has a senior citizen volunteer in her classroom during her reading block. This person listens and coaches as students reread their EIR stories and provides assistance during students' independent work time. Leah also has an educational assistant who works with ELL students.

Average and above-average readers typically have one or two follow-up activities to the whole-group lesson and one or two follow-up activities to their small-group lesson during their independent work time. The below-average readers typically have two or three different activities to work on during their independent work time. All students also read for 25 to 30 minutes a day from fiction and nonfiction books of their choosing. Here is what her schedule might look like:

Leah's Daily Groups

9:00–9:40	Whole-Group Lesson
9:40–9:55	Small-Group 1
9:55–10:15	Small-Group 2
10:15–10:30	Small-Group 3
10:30–10:50	EIR Lesson

Independent Activities in Leah Davis' Classroom

Independent activities Leah structures for her students include the following:

▶ After engaging in prereading activities and a lesson on cause-and-effect relationships for the basal reader story, *Officer Buckle and Gloria,* in a whole-group lesson, students read the story on their own, answer high-level teacher-generated questions about the story with a partner, write the meanings of vocabulary words from the story in their own words, write in their journal about the time they had a problem with a friend, and put sticky notes in their book where they found cause-and-effect relationships.

▶ After listening to the teacher read *The Relatives Came* by Cynthia Rylant, students read a just-right book and write down connections they make to their story on sticky notes.

▶ After a whole-group lesson on making inferences related to a *George and Martha* story by James Marshall, students complete a teacher-generated sheet on making inferences related to the story. They also write in their journal about a rule they have at their home, which is a topic in the *George and Martha* story. Leah asks them to write about what they think about this rule and give reasons for their answers.

▶ After listening to Leah read a story about Ruby Bridges, students make connections by writing about a quality of Ruby Bridges they would choose for themselves and explaining why they made this choice. Leach reminds them to make connections between self and the text.

▶ After listening to their teacher read *The Patchwork Quilt* by Valerie Flourney, the students use vocabulary words from the story as they summarize the story. Leah reminds them to be sure they show her they know what the words mean in their sentences.

Diane Swanson's Daily Reading Block Schedule

Diane has a 120-minute reading block each day. She spends about 30 to 40 minutes a day on a whole-group lesson and about 20 minutes with each of two guided reading groups and two EIR groups. A Title 1 teacher comes into the classroom to teach the guided reading lessons for the two groups of EIR students. Diane has an educational assistant in her room who works with three students on work word that is in addition to their guided reading group lesson.

Average and above-average readers spend about 60 minutes a day on independent learning activities, and below-average readers spend about 40 minutes a day on independent learning activities. The educational assistant also listens to EIR students reread their stories and provides assistance to all students as they are engaged in independent work activities. Here is how her time is scheduled:

Diane's Daily Groups

9:00–9:35	Whole-Group Lesson
9:35–9:55	Small-Groups 1 (taught by Diane) and 2 (taught by Title I teacher)
9:35–9:55	Small-Groups 3 (taught by Diane) and 4 (taught by Title 1 teacher)
10:20–10:40	EIR Lesson for Group 2 (taught by Diane)
10:40–11:00	EIR Lesson for Group 4 (taught by Diane)

Independent Activities in Diane Swanson's Classroom

Students complete independent work activities according to a five-day reading ticket that allows them to decide when to complete required activities during the week. Activities include word work; listening and responding to stories with big ideas on tape; doing research on informational topics tied to the second-grade social studies and science curricula, using books and the Internet; completing open-ended response sheets and graphic organizers related to books read in whole- and small-group lessons; participating in book clubs; and reading for pleasure. The average and above-average readers typically complete three or four different activities and the below-average readers two or three activities during their independent work time. Example activities from Diane's lessons include:

▶ After reading a story about the first Thanksgiving and discussing how to find answers to questions, Diane has students select a book at their reading level on an animal of their choosing and do research to find answers to three questions on an open-ended response sheet. She asks: What does your animal eat? Where does it live? and What is one interesting thing you learned about your animal?

▶ After reading a story, *The Great Ball Game,* in their basal readers, Diane has students write in their journal the advice they would give to the birds and the animals in the story.

▶ After summarizing a story in a small-group lesson, Diane has students write a summary for the story in their own words.

▶ After a lesson on making connections, Diane gives students 5 minutes to write about their independent reading in their journals. The teacher-generated prompt is: What did your reading remind you of? Explain with details.

▶ After working on book talks of stories by Jan Brett, students practice giving their book talks with a partner.

▶ Students read the newspaper with help from the educational assistant and write about one new piece of information they learned from their reading to share later.

▶ Working with the educational assistant, students do research on the arctic reading books and reading on the Internet.

▶ After a reading about a sequence of events, students write about how to make a pie.

▶ Students read for at least 100 minutes a week from their book boxes.

More Suggestions for Challenging Independent Activities

Independent work time can be one of the most academically powerful junctures of the school day, because it's when students actually practice being the motivated, self-regulated learners we want them to be. The following additional activities sufficiently engage and challenge second graders so they are less likely to go off-task into unproductive or disruptive behavior. Ensuring that independent time works well is crucial because it is one goal we're after—creating independent, motivated learners.

What factors prevent second graders from learning to read and learning to enjoy reading? Low-level tasks are one major factor. Research by Pressley and colleagues (2003) found that teaching behaviors that undermined academic motivation in primary-grade classrooms included tasks with low-task difficulty in which students were asked to complete activities that were too easy, required low cognitive effort, and demanded little of them (80). Also, students in these classrooms were given activities that were uninspiring, boring, simplistic, and lacked excitement or provided stimulation to students.

In my many visits to second-grade classrooms over the ten years I worked with schools on schoolwide reading improvement (Taylor et al. 2005; Taylor 2010c), I often saw students engaged in primarily low-level tasks during independent work time. Typically, students in these classrooms were completing worksheets or workbook pages, coloring, and rereading stories more times than were warranted. Also, these activities often could be completed in much less time than the time allowed, which only compounded the likelihood that students dawdled, got off-task, chatted with students near them, or wandered around the room.

At the other end of the spectrum, on my schools visits, I also often went into classrooms in which students were participating in many tasks requiring high-level thinking and collaboration during independent work time. The levels of student engagement and the numbers of happy faces and excited eyes of these students as compared to the children in classrooms with less motivating activities were striking. Students typically had three or four activities to complete that kept them meaningfully engaged and working at a continuous, efficient pace. With enough to do and with interesting things to work on, they did not get off-task. Most important, they appeared to be happy, self-regulated learners.

These observations are supported by research of Pressley and colleagues (2003) on tasks that enhanced academic motivation in primary-grade classrooms. They found that teachers had motivated learners when they engaged them in cooperative learning and high-order, critical, and creative thinking. These teachers also used engaging and interesting texts that piqued students' curiosity, got them excited about their learning, and involved them in excellent literature.

Below examples of independent work time activities to engage students and advance their literacy abilities are provided. Independent student response sheets that go with some of these suggestions are in Figures 8-1 to 8-13. These figures are also on the DVD as reproducibles.

Activities That Support Word Recognition

See words for word sorts in *Words Their Way* by Bear et al., 2004.

▶ To reinforce students' knowledge of symbol sound correspondence that you have recently taught in guided reading groups, have them complete word sorts with a partner. For example, if you have recently taught a group that there are two common sounds for *a*, the short and long sounds, you could have them sort words containing /a/ with the CVC and CVCe patterns. To get practice reading words containing particular phonic elements, students should read the words that have been sorted.

See words for word families in *Words Their Way* by Bear et al., 2004.

▶ To reinforce students' knowledge of symbol sound correspondence that you have recently taught in guided reading groups, have them write words that fall into various word families with a partner. A skilled reader (volunteer, educational assistant, older student helper) should check words generated (e.g., so that *bight* for *bite* is not written under words with the *-ight* pattern). To get practice reading words containing particular phonic elements, students should read the words they have been generated.

- Have students work with a partner or small group to generate words in a Making Words activity for which the directions have been written on a card by the teacher. To get practice reading words containing particular phonic elements, students should read words generated and sort words into word families.

- If your school's spelling curriculum uses weekly spelling lists and tests, have students practice spelling misspelled words from their weekly spelling lists after you have given students a pretest and they have self-corrected misspelled words. Word lists should be differentiated based on students' reading and spelling abilities.

Activities That Support Fluency

- With a partner, have students reread stories from their guided reading group or EIR lesson. Students should coach one another on difficult words. See Chapter 3 for prompts for students to use during partner reading.

- Have students reread stories from their guided reading group or EIR lesson with a volunteer, educational assistant, or older student helper (who coaches as students get stuck on words they cannot decode instantly).

- Have students reread stories in their book box. They should list books reread for fluency, and self-rate their fluency on books read (see Figure 8-1).

- Have students read new books for pleasure. They should log books they read (see Figure 8-2).

tips

See *Phonics They Use: Words for Reading and Writing*, 5th ed., Cunningham, 2009, for more on Making Words.

tips

For additional suggestions on fluency, see *The Fluent Reader: Oral Reading Strategies for Building Word Recognition, Fluency, and Comprehension*, Rasinski, 2003.

See the DVD for full-size versions of all the forms in this chapter.

Practicing and Rating My Reading Fluency

Name _____ Date _____

Title _____

_____

I read my story _____ times.

a. My reading rate was: Good 😊 Okay 😐 Could Be Better 🙁

b. My phrasing was: Good 😊 Okay 😐 Could Be Better 🙁

c. My expression was: Good 😊 Okay 😐 Could Be Better 🙁

I want to work on a, b, or c (circle one).

Figure 8-1 Practicing and Rating My Reading Fluency

Log for Independent Pleasure Reading

Name _____ Date _____

Book Title	Date	Start page	End page	My ideas are:

Figure 8-2 Log for Independent Pleasure Reading

For additional suggestions see *Bringing Words to Life: Robust Vocabulary Instruction*, Beck, McKeown, and Kucan, 2002

Activities That Support Vocabulary

▶ On sticky notes or in a vocabulary journal, have students write down interesting, unknown, or newly learned words that come from the books they are reading. Students can share words and possible meanings with the teacher in whole- or small-group lesson or by turning vocabulary journal in to teacher, or with a volunteer, educational assistant, or older classroom helper.

▶ Have students complete a concept map or web of juicy words identified by their teacher from books they are reading (see Figure 8-3).

For more suggestions see *Comprehension Shouldn't Be Silent*, Kelley and Clausen-Grace, 2007.

Reciprocal Teaching at Work: Strategies for Improving Reading Comprehension, Oczkus, 2003.

QAR Now, Raphael, Highfield, and Au, 2006.

Activities That Support Comprehension: Skills and Strategies

Have students:

▶ Read books to practice comprehension skills and strategies. Examples of open-ended response sheets include the following: cause-effect chart (Figure 8-4), topic map (Figure 8-5), comparison chart (Figure 8-6), fact/opinion chart (Figure 8-7), summary sheet for narrative text (Figure 8-8), summary sheet for informational text (Figure 8-9), comprehension monitoring sheet (Figure 8-10), and reciprocal teaching sheet (Figure 8-11).

▶ Write questions as they read of after they are finished reading. Question types include the following: clarifying, main idea, summary, and interpretive evaluative/critical literacy.

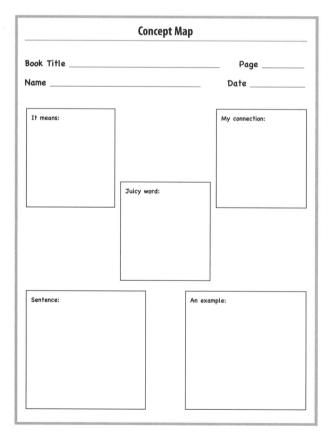

Figure 8-3 Concept Map

Cause-Effect Chart

Book _____

Name _____ Date _____

This Happened (Cause)	On Page	That Made This Happen (Effect)	On Page	My Ideas

Figure 8-4 Cause-Effect Chart

Topic Map

Name _____ Date _____

Food:

Habitat:

My animal (topic) is:

Babies:

Appearance:

Interesting facts:

Figure 8-5 Topic Map

Comparison Chart

Book Titles _____

Name _____

Date _____

	Animal 1: Wolf	Similar (S) or Different (D)	Animal 2: Coyote
Appearance	90 pounds	D	45 pounds
Food	Little animals	S	Little animals
Habitat	Woods	S	Woods
Babies			
Interesting Facts	Travel in a pack	D	Travel alone

Figure 8-6 Comparison Chart

Fact-Opinion Chart

Name _____ Book Title _____

Idea (sentence)	Page	Fact (F) or Opinion (O)	Why?

Figure 8-7 Fact-Opinion Chart

Narrative Summary Sheet

Name _____ Book Title _____

Beginning (who, where, problem):	Middle (events):
End (solution):	Author's message:

New Words

Write two words that you did not know or that you found interesting and what you think they mean if you can.

Word	Page	Meaning

Figure 8-8 Narrative Summary Sheet

Summary Sheet for Informational Text

Name _____

Summarize the informational text you read. Write in complete sentences.

	Main Idea	Important Details
Part 1		
Part 2		
Part 3		

New Words

Write two words that you did not know or that you found interesting and what you think they mean if you can.

Word	Page	Meaning

Figure 8-9 Summary Sheet for Informational Text

Note-Taking Sheet on Comprehension Monitoring

Name _____ Date _____

Word or Idea That Confused Me	Page	Notes

Figure 8-10 Note-Taking Sheet on Comprehension Monitoring

Sheet for Practicing Reciprocal Teaching Strategies

Name _____ Book Title _____

A. Summarizing the Story
Tell about what you read in one or two sentences (for pages _____).

B. Generating Questions from the Story
Ask two important questions about what you read:

    1. (from page ____)

    2. (From page ____)

C. Clarifying—Check for Understanding
Note other ideas that you have questions about or vocabulary that you need to understand better.

    1. (from page ____)

    2. (from page _____)

D. Predicting
Write a prediction about what you think will be in the next section of the text (if a prediction comes to mind).

Repeat Steps A–D for the next section of the text.

Figure 8-11 Example of a Sheet for Practicing Reciprocal Teaching Strategies

Activities That Support Comprehension: Learning New Information

Have students:

▶ Read books to learn new information.

▶ Read on the Internet to learn more information.

▶ Read about topics in social studies and science curriculum. Teachers, the media specialist, or volunteers could locate existing books at the school or purchase books (with school funds, funds from PTA, funds or local businesses) at various reading levels that covered topics in social studies and science curriculum for grade 2.

▶ Prepare and give an oral presentation (Figure 8-12) with a partner, triad, on independently.

▶ Prepare a written report (use Figure 8-5 for an outline). After reading about a topic students could write reports on this topic with a partner, triad, or independently. Other topics for writing after reading include: procedures, recounting an event, explanation, or persuasion.

▶ Write down words to share (vocabulary) and write about them (Figure 8-3) after independent reading on topics of interest.

For more suggestions, see

Reading and Writing Informational Text in the Primary Grades, Duke and Bennett-Armistead, 2003.

Informational Text in K–3 Classrooms: Helping Children Read and Write, Kletsien and Dreher, 2005.

Note-Taking Sheet for an Oral Book Report

Name _____ Date _____

A. Beginning: Characters, Setting, Problem

B. Events

C. Solution to Problem

D. Author's Message

Share Your Ideas

1. Tell about a part you liked and why.

2. Tell how this is like your life and why.

New Words

Write two words that you did not know or that you found interesting and what you think they mean if you can.

Word	Page	Meaning

Note-Taking Sheet for Vocabulary and High-Level Questions to Discuss at a Book Club

Question Sheet for Narrative Books

Book Title:

Names:

Write two juicy questions about the story (why, how, what do you think?)

1.

2.

Share Your Ideas

1. Tell about a part you liked or didn't like and why.

2. Tell how this is like your life and why.

New Words

Write two words that you did not know or that you found interesting and what you think they mean if you can.

Figure 8-12 Note-Taking Sheet for an Oral Book Report

Figure 8-13 Note-Taking Sheet for Vocabulary and High-Level Questions to Discuss at Book Club

For more suggestions see

Book Club: A Literature-Based Curriculum. 2d ed. Raphael, Pardo, and Highfield, 2002.

Moving Forward with Literature Circles, Day, Spiegel, McLellan, and Brown, 2002.

Critical Literacy and Writer's Workshop, Heffernan, 2004.

Using Literature to Enhance Content Area Instruction: A Guide for K–5 Teachers, Olness, 2007.

Comprehension from the Ground Up, Taberski, 2011.

For more suggestions see *What Should I Read Aloud?.* Anderson, 2007.

Literature on the Child, 7th ed., Galda and Cullinan, 2010.

Activities That Support Comprehension: Talking and Writing About Text

▶ Students can work on the following after they have had modeling and coaching lessons from the teacher.

▶ Participate in literature circles—learn routines, read and take notes, and share (Figure 8-13).

▶ Respond to literature (Figures 8-12 and 8-13).

▶ Prepare and give a book report (Figure 8-12).

▶ Engage in critical literacy, in which students evaluate, express, discuss, and write ideas related to an issue they have read about.

Activities That Support Reading for Pleasure

Have students:

▶ Read books from different genre for 20 to 30 minutes a day. After reading, have students complete reading log (see Figure 8-2).

▶ Read different books from a favorite author.

▶ Share favorite books in a book sharing club.

▶ Write about favorite books on cards for a book file that other students can look through for book suggestions.

Independent work time is an important component of teachers' overall classroom reading program. Students spend a considerable amount of time working on their own or with others while teachers work with small, guided reading groups. It is crucial that students are actively engaged in interesting, challenging learning activities that meet their needs and move them forward in literacy abilities during this independent work time. However, it is easy for these independent learning activities to become routine, undifferentiated, unnecessary practice, and not motivating or challenging to students. It is easy for students to get off-task or to spend much longer on assigned activities than is needed just to fill up the time.

Teachers often find it is helpful to share ideas to help each other plan for effective independent learning activities as part of the effective reading instruction they provide in their classrooms.

For more on effective, motivating reading instruction and assessment in general: *Classroom Reading Assessment: Making Sense of What Students Know and Do,* Paratore and McCormack, 2007.

Reading Instruction That Works: The Case for Balanced Teaching, 3rd ed., Pressley et al., 2006.

On Solid Ground: Strategies for Teaching Reading K–3, Taberski, 2000.

Creating an EIR Community

Early Intervention in Reading is a powerful approach for accelerating children's reading development for struggling readers. EIR is not a curriculum tied to specific books, but rather a repertoire of teaching strategies that require teacher reflection and considerable skill. Professional learning sessions are critical. Support from a building facilitator and outreach to parents are also important.

1. Teachers need to work with colleagues during their first year of teaching EIR lessons.

First and foremost, over many years, I have found that teachers experience more success with their students when they regularly participate in monthly meetings with colleagues to discuss EIR during the first year they are teaching the lessons. Together, teachers can clarify procedures, share successes, and help one another solve problems. Taking on EIR and weaving it in to effective whole-group and small-group instruction amounts to highly differentiated teaching—not an easy thing to achieve.

In a research study on effective reading practices (Taylor et al. 2000), the most effective schools had a collaborative model for delivering reading instruction in which struggling readers received a second, 30-minute small-group reading

intervention each day to accelerate their literacy learning. Therefore, I strongly recommend that classroom teachers, Title 1 and other reading resource teachers, ELL teachers, and special education teachers meet together in these monthly EIR professional learning experiences. Teachers will not solve all of their students' reading problems unless they work collaboratively. Classroom teachers know their students the best and must be part of the solution.

2. Teachers need to get help from others on scheduling the monthly meetings and sustaining the one-on-one coaching conferences that are an essential piece of EIR.

If numerous teachers are learning about and teaching EIR in the same year, it is extremely helpful if a school has a building facilitator to provide support. This person can take responsibility for securing EIR books and materials, for scheduling of professional learning sessions, for establishing the one-on-one coaching component of EIR by aides, volunteers, or older students, and for problem solving as issues arise.

See the DVD for full-size versions of all the forms in this chapter.

3. Teachers need to do outreach to parents/caregivers, so that they can help their children practice reading at home.

Parents have a critical role to play in EIR. Children take their EIR story home at the end of the third day so they can read to their parents. In Figure 9-1 is a Reading at Home sheet for parents to sign. (Note: This figure and all the figures in this chapter are supplied as full-sized reproducibles on the DVD.) In Figure 9-2, there are coaching prompts for parents to use when listening to their children read. Also, in the supplemental resources on the DVD, there are take-home activities based on the EIR stories that the parents, or an older sibling, other relative, or neighbor, should help their children with at home. Parents should sign the EIR at-home sheets and have their children bring them back to school.

To introduce these activities to parents, a sample letter you can send home explaining EIR is provided in Figure 9-3. Also, at the beginning of the school year, you can invite parents to an "EIR Party," perhaps at the school's back-to-school-night event, in which you explain the materials that will be coming home and the importance of parents' involvement in these activities. You can demonstrate the coaching prompts for parents at this time. Also, you may want to show parents a video of yourself coaching children in their EIR group. Children can come along to the party and eat cookies to make it a festive event.

For parents who can't make it to school, you can send home a video of yourself reading with their child and coaching as the child is stuck on difficult words. One teacher reported taping each child in

---

Reading at Home Sheet

Date _____

_____ has read the book
(student's name)

_____ to me _____ times.
(book name)

Comments:_____

_____

_____

_____

_____

_____

_____

_____

_____
(parent's/caregiver's signature)

Figure 9-1 Reading at Home Sheet

Tips for Reading with Beginning Readers at Home

In EIR, teachers help children learn to depend on themselves to figure out hard words. To work on this at home, try one of the following prompts or tips when a young reader gets stuck or makes a mistake:

1. Wait and see if they work it out.

2. Say, "Try that again."

3. Say, "Look at the picture."

4. Say, "Think about what would make sense."

5. Say, "Sound it out."

If the word is a hard one, you may want to tell the child the word. But if the word is an easy one, try one or more of these tips listed before you give the child the word.

Figure 9-2 Tips for Reading with Beginning Readers at Home

Parent/Guardian Information Letter

Dear Parent/Guardian,

To help maximize your child's success in reading, we are using supplementary reading lessons called Early Intervention in Reading (EIR). EIR will help your child by using a different approach to experience reading success. We are excited about it!

We want to emphasize that we really need your involvement. How can you help? Watch for a book and/or take-home activities your child will bring home. Be sure to listen to your child read the story and help with the take-home activities. Return the take-home activity with your signature. Research shows, *"Kids who read the most, read the best!"*

This is the way we teach EIR:

1. The teacher reads the book to the group.

2. The teacher guides students as they read the story and then discuss it.

3. Three to five words are selected by the teacher to work on decoding.

4. Children write a sentence about the story, based on a question the teacher has asked.

5. The child practices reading the book at home.

Remember: Listen to your child read the book and assist with the take-home activities. Please help your child return the completed take-home activities page with your signature.

Thank you for your continued support as we work together to help your child have success in reading.

Sincerely,

Figure 9-3 Parent/Guardian Information Letter

November and May and then giving the recording to the parents at the end of the year. Another strategy teachers have used for involving parents is inviting them to school to see EIR lessons in action.

Overview of the Monthly EIR Meetings

At monthly meetings (about 60–80 minutes in duration), teachers learning to teach EIR lessons can work together to clarify procedures, share successes, and problem-solve. Teachers can also hone their abilities to coach children to use word-recognition strategies, depend on themselves, and deepen reading comprehension through answering thought-provoking questions. Meetings should begin in August or September and continue through May. Again, this meeting might take place on a single day or be spread out over several days during the month. In the first 10 to 15 minutes of the meeting, the group can focus on sharing ideas and concerns related to EIR lessons. Reviewing and discussing grade-level procedures and videos clips of effective practice will take about 30 to 40 minutes. By November, the video segments can come from teachers' own teaching of EIR lessons. A monthly meeting overview guide is in Table 9-1.

In August, read and discuss Chapters 1 and 2 with the group. Chapter 1 reviews effective classroom reading instruction, and provides an overview of the theory and research behind EIR instruction for struggling readers. Chapter 2

Monthly Meeting Overview

August/September	Review Chapters 1, 2, 3, 4, and 8. Discuss instructional procedures and watch video clips on the DVD that go with Chapter 3
	Review fall assessments in Chapter 7
	Prepare for October meeting
October	Status report on EIR teaching (discuss how your EIR groups are going; review procedures as questions arise)
	Review video-sharing procedures
	Discuss one-on-one coaching
	Review EIR procedures
	Prepare for November meeting
November	Status report on EIR teaching
	Status report of one-on-one coaching
	Review video-viewing procedures
	Discuss grade-level procedures
	Engage in video sharing
	Prepare for December meeting
December	Status report on EIR teaching
	Discuss one-on-one coaching
	Group Activity: Book Lesson Share
	Grade-level procedures
	Group Activity: Discuss children's self-correction abilities
	Video sharing
	Prepare for January meeting
January	Status report on EIR teaching
	Coaching for comprehension
	Status report on one-on-one coaching
	Discuss transition procedures—Chapter 5
	Video viewing/sharing
	Prepare for February meeting
February	Status of children's progress
	Discuss transition phase
	Review procedures for oral reading analysis
	Video sharing
	Prepare for March meeting
March	Status of children's progress
	Decoding multisyllabic words strategy
	Discuss oral reading analysis and instruction
	Video sharing
	Prepare for April meeting
April	Status of children's progress
	Reflection on grade-level procedures
	Review spring assessment procedures
May (if time permits, or at a grade-level meeting)	Status of children's progress
	Discuss results of assessments
	Review year and discuss plans for next year

Table 9-1 Monthly Meeting Overview for Teachers Using Basic Grade 2 EIR

shares sample lessons for all students from teachers who also teach EIR lessons. You may also want to read and discuss Chapter 8, which details how to fit EIR into your daily literacy block as well as how to make sure your students have motivating activities to work on while you are working with EIR and guided groups. See Taylor, forthcoming, on effective reading instruction and school-based professional learning communities.

Additionally, in August or early September, you should begin to review the EIR procedures in Chapter 3. During your September and October meetings, review together the three-day EIR routines in detail. You can revisit certain aspects of the EIR procedures as questions arise in later meetings.

Some teachers report uneasiness about "doing the EIR procedures correctly" and want to delay getting started. However, I always tell teachers not to worry if they are doing things "just right" at first; they will get better at using EIR strategies over time. What is important is to get started with EIR lessons as close to October 1 as possible. Most children who would benefit from EIR need the intervention all year. They should get started with reading intervention lessons that make them feel successful as soon as possible at the beginning of the school year before feelings of discouragement about reading set in.

Beginning in November, I recommend you incorporate video sharing into your monthly EIR meetings. To do this, teachers take turns bringing in a five- to eight-minute video clip of their EIR teaching to share and discuss. These video-sharing experiences give teachers the opportunity to reflect on and discuss their practice. So often, professional development focuses on curriculum lessons tied to a teacher's manual or the proper use of new materials. Teachers are rarely given the opportunity, with the help of colleagues, to think, talk about, and enhance their teaching practices.

The focus of the video sharing should be:

▶ What the children are doing well or what strengths they are demonstrating in the EIR lesson

▶ What the teacher is doing well to foster strategy use, independence, and success in the children

▶ What else the teacher might have done to foster strategy use, independence, and success

Through EIR ongoing professional learning sessions teachers will improve their coaching abilities. Focusing on coaching and working at it collaboratively helps teachers understand that coaching children to become independent is not easy. However, teachers also learn that coaching is something they can master, with the end result of having more children in your classrooms reading well by the end of the school year. Video-sharing procedures are described in greater detail in Figure 9-4 on page 129.

Agendas for Monthly Meetings

September Meeting (70–75 min.)

Recommended activities for professional learning in September include the following:

Review Chapters 1 and 2 (10–15 min.)

First, in September, discuss any remaining questions or issues you have related to Chapters 1 and 2. You may also wish to talk about Chapter 8 if your group chose to read that chapter as well.

Discuss Instructional Procedures in Chapter 3 and Book Selection in Chapter 4 (35–40 min.)

Carefully work through Chapter 3 covers the basic grade 2 EIR routines. Also, I recommend that you watch the related video clips on the DVD. Discuss book selection and the books you plan to use in your EIR lesson.

Review Assessment Procedures in Chapter 7 (20 min.)

Review the fall assessment procedures described in Chapter 7. Select passages from an informal reading inventory that you will all use in the fall assessments to determine which students need EIR lessons.

Prepare for October Meeting (5 min.)

Briefly review what needs to be done before the October meeting:

> Complete assessment of students and identify which need EIR. Don't worry if you aren't quite sure about your placement decisions. You can ask questions in October and make changes then.

> Start your EIR lessons as early as possible. You will get a lot more out of the October meeting if you have already started to teach EIR lessons. You should jot down notes on this instruction so you have a chance to share experiences and to get questions answered at the October meeting.

Often, people say they aren't ready to get started yet, but I tell them to simply "take the plunge!" You will get better at teaching EIR lessons as the year moves along. The best way to learn about EIR instructional strategies is to start teaching EIR lessons. Good luck!

October Meeting (65–70 min.)

This month you will continue to learn and talk about procedures in grade-level groups. Additionally, you need to prepare for video sharing, which should begin in November. Begin organizing for your one-on-one reading coaching.

Status Report on EIR teaching (10 min.)

Across the group, take turns reporting on how things have gone so far with the initial teaching of EIR lessons.

Review Video-Sharing Procedures (20 min.)

Each person should bring one video to share in November, December, or January and a second in February, March, or April. Share one or two videos each month. To learn about video sharing, see Figure 9-4.

The basic approach to video sharing was developed for the Early Intervention in Reading (EIR) Professional Development Program but has also been used in other teacher professional development venues. Each video-sharing segment should take no more than 15 minutes.

Prior to coming to your study group, do the following:

a. Videotape the lesson segment you selected. It should be 5 minutes long.

b. Answer the following three video-sharing questions based on your video:

- What were things the children were able to do related to your focus area? What things were going well?

- What was the teacher doing to help children develop and be successful related to your focus area?

- What else could have been done to foster development and success related to your focus area?

When you share the video at an EIR session, do the following:

1. Share 1 minute of background about the lesson.

2. Tell the group something you would like their help with and thus want them to pay attention to while watching the video clip.

Engaging in Video Sharing

The basic approach to video sharing was developed for the Early Intervention in Reading (EIR) Professional Development Program but has also been used with success in other teacher professional development venues (Taylor 2010c). Each video-sharing segment should take no more than 15 minutes. Focus on students' strategy use, independence, and success.

Prior to coming to your study group, do the following:

  a. Videotape the lesson segment you selected. It should be 5 minutes long.

  b. Answer the following three video-sharing questions based on your video:

    ▶ What were things the children were able to do related to your focus area? What things were going well?

    ▶ What was the teacher doing to help children develop and be successful related to your focus area?

    ▶ What else could have been done to foster development and success related to your focus area?

When you share the video at an EIR session, do the following:

  1. Share 1 minute of background about the lesson.

  2. Tell the group something you would like their help with.

  3. View the video with the group.

  4. Break into groups of three to review the three video-sharing questions. Take notes on things the children did well, things the teacher in the clip did well in getting children to develop and experience success related to the focus area, and offer suggestions for things that might have been done differently to help the children develop and experience success related to the focus area.

  5. Discuss the video clip as a larger group. (View the video again if group feels it needs to.) The facilitator will ask the three video-sharing questions to the group. Members from the groups of three can share points that they wish to share. Notes from small groups should be given to the teacher who brought the video clip of her teaching.

  6. The teacher who brought the clip should ask for their ideas related to item 2 above.

Remember, this is first and foremost a learning activity in which colleagues are helping one another improve their skills as coaches. At an EIR session, sign up to show video clips of their teaching for a specific topic—one part of one day's lesson (see form in Figure 9-5).

Figure 9-4 Engaging in Video Sharing

3. View the video with the group.

4. Break into groups of three to review the three video-sharing questions. Take notes on things the children did well, things the teacher in the clip did well in getting children to develop related to the focus area and to experience success related to this focus area, and offer suggestions for things that might have been done differently to help the children develop and experience success related to the focus area.

5. Discuss the video clip as a larger group. (View the video again if group feels it needs to.) The facilitator will ask the three video-sharing questions to the group. Members from the groups of three can share points that they wish to share. Notes from small groups should be given to the teacher who brought the video clip of her teaching.

6. The teacher who brought the clip should ask for their ideas related to item 2.

Remember, this is first and foremost a learning activity in which colleagues are helping one another improve their skills as coaches. At an EIR session, sign up to show a video clips of their teaching for a specific topic—one part of one day's lesson (See form in Figure 9–5).

People should sign up for the video sharing in October. (See Figure 9-5, Video Sharing Sign-Up Sheet.) If you have more than six teachers in your group, break into grade-level groups of three to five members for the video sharing part of the meeting. With six members in a video-sharing group, you will watch two videos a month. With three members in a video-sharing group, you will watch one video a month.

Video Sharing—Sign-Up Sheet for Grade 2

Month	Teacher	Description of Video
November		Teacher models word-recognition strategies as she reads book on Day 1
		Sentence writing
December		Making words activity
		Teachers coaches as children read story on Day 2
		Coaching for comprehension
January		Teacher coaches as children read story on Day 3 or Transition
		Making Words
		Coaching for comprehension
February		Teacher coaches or takes an oral reading check on Day 1
		Transition
		Sentence writing
March		Coaching for comprehension
		Transition
		Oral Reading Analysis
April		Coaching for comprehension
		Transition

Figure 9-5 Video Sharing—Sign- Up Sheet for Grade 2

Discuss One-on-One Coaching (10 min.)

Discuss the status of the one-on-one coaching piece of EIR or the plans for getting this component in place as soon as possible. One-on-one coaches might be educational assistants, classroom volunteers, or older students who are classroom helpers who receive training on how to be a coach. (See the section on training coaches later in this chapter and in Figures 9-6 to 9-10 and on the DVD.)

To get maximum results with EIR, one-on-one coaching should occur on a regular basis. Children need the opportunity to practice reading with no other child next to them calling out a word they don't know. Also, individual children need the chance to show themselves what they are able to work on reading independently. Even if you are not responsible for training the one-on-one coaches, you should look through the information presented on this topic so you understand the training the coaches have received. Also, as the classroom teacher, you need to supervise the one-on-one coaches and give constructive feedback as needed.

Review EIR Procedures (20–25 min.)

Refer to your notes about your EIR lessons and raise any questions you have; other members in your group may have the answers. You may want to return to the sections in Chapter 3, on grade-level routines for these answers. It may be helpful to consider the following observations I have about EIR lessons and students in October.

▶ In the fall as I visit second-grade classrooms, I am struck by how much more the children know than the first-grade children even though the second graders in EIR are not yet reading much on their own.

▶ By November, I see children doing well with practices such as only using their finger as a guide while reading if they need to or trying different strategies to decode words. I see a few children who still haven't caught on to the alphabetic principle, but this is uncommon. I also see children somewhere in between these two ends of the continuum; for these children, I find I especially need to remind them to use context (What would make sense in the story?) to help them figure out a word. Many children need help learning how to use the short vowel chart. Soon they should not need to use the chart but will know the short vowel sounds by thinking about the words on the chart.

▶ Review and discuss the following video clips related to modeling and coaching in word recognition: Videos 2 and 9.

▶ Review Video 11. With sentence writing, the teacher does an excellent job of coaching the children to come up with letters for sounds instead of just telling them how to spell words they are trying to write in their sentences.

Prepare for November Meeting (5 min.)

For the November meeting, one or two people per small group should be bringing in short video clips to share predetermined segments of EIR lessons. (Refer back to Figure 9-5.) An example of a segment would be Steps 1, 2, 3, or 4 from Days 1, 2, or 3.

November Meeting (60–75 min.)

Status Report on EIR Teaching (10 min.)

At this time in the year, I am already impressed with teachers' excellent coaching when I visit classrooms. Share things you have noticed about your coaching.

One-on-One Coaching, Status Report (5 min.)

Questions About the Video Sharing (5 min.)

Discuss Grade-Level Procedures (20 min.)

By now, you are probably feeling more comfortable with the EIR routine. However, in November, I often have to remind teachers that timing is a key factor in EIR lessons. Be sure you are getting to all of the parts of a lesson. Also, move toward the goal of only spending three days on a lesson. Discuss strategies for getting through all steps of a lesson. If there are parts of the EIR routine that you want to review, return to the relevant sections of Chapter 3 and the corresponding video clips.

Observations I typically have in November include the following:

▶ Children are very motivated to write. Discuss what you have noticed about the children's writing.

▶ You should be in EIR Level B books and into Making Words instead of the Sound Box activity. If you need to review Making Words, return to Chapter 3 and discuss Videos 5 and 6. It is important to remember the word-sorting portion of Making Words helps the children learn to decode by onset and rime.

Video Sharing (15–30 min.)

Share one or two videos, depending on the size of your group. Many people are nervous about video sharing, but it gets a lot easier by the second time around. In May, on EIR evaluations I have collected over the years, many teachers tell me the video sharing was one of the most valuable parts of professional learning sessions. So, I encourage you to hang in there with the video-sharing experience.

Prepare for December Meeting (5 min.)

For the December meeting, one or two people (depending on the size of your group) should bring in short video clips to share predetermined segments of EIR lessons.

December Meeting (65–80 min.)

Status Report on EIR Teaching (10 min.)

Now that you know the EIR procedures, it is a good time to reflect on your coaching for comprehension. Keep a list of the questions you are asking your students, jot down notes on your questioning practices, and bring them to share at the meeting next month. The following are some questions to get you thinking about your questioning and coaching for comprehension.

▶ Are you asking follow-up questions to get children to clarify what they are saying or to elaborate on their ideas?

▶ Are you giving children enough wait time?

▶ Are you coaching quiet children to talk (e.g., those who like to say, "I don't know") instead of just moving on to another child?

▶ Are you asking some questions that are based on a concept in the story but that leave the story behind and instead relate to children's lives? (For example, What things do you usually do before you go to bed like the girl did in *Ten, Nine, Eight*?)

▶ Are your questions thought provoking and meaningful to the children? (For example, after reading *Rain*, do you ask something like, "Tell about times you like the rain and times you do not. Explain why." Why is this a more thought-provoking question than, "Have you ever seen a rainbow? How did you feel?")

One-on-One Coaching, Status Report (5 min.)

It is very important that this component of EIR be up and running. If possible, try to observe your one-on-one coaches so you can give them feedback.

Group Activity (10 min.)

With a partner, generate some good coaching for comprehension questions from the books you will be using in future EIR lessons. Share these questions with the larger group.

Grade-Level Procedures (20 min.)

At this time of year, I often remind second-grade teachers to focus on their prompting for and praising of self-corrections. By getting children to notice when they need to self-correct, we are helping them to become more independent readers. As children start to self-correct on a more regular basis, be sure you are giving them enough wait time to do so. If you are too quick to prompt them to self-correct, you are not giving them the chance to notice when something they've read just isn't right.

If you are meeting late in January, or if your children are ready now, you should go to Chapter 5, which details the transition stage to independent reading. By January at the latest, begin to use the transition procedures with books at Level E. With the transition procedures, children read stories they have never read before. An important part of EIR is getting children away from the repeated reading approach that has been successful for them because it is not the same as picking up an unfamiliar book and decoding it successfully.

Group Activity (10 min.)

Discuss children's self-correction abilities. Brainstorm ways to help those students who are not yet self-correcting often.

Video Sharing (15–30 min.)

Engage in video sharing.

Grade 2 Accelerated Procedures (30 min.)

If you have students who would benefit from the the grade 2 accelerated procedures, work through Chapter 6. If you don't finish, complete the chapter on your own before the January meeting. It is important that you have a chance to discuss the procedures and ask and answer questions with others as they arise.

Start the grade 2 accelerated routines prior to the January meeting, if you can. You will get a lot more out of the January meeting if you do. Jot down notes about your lessons so that the group can answer your questions you can share your experiences at the next meeting.

Prepare for January Meeting (2 min.)

For the January meeting, two people per small group should bring in short video clips to share a predetermined piece of an EIR lesson. Read about transition procedures in Chapter 5.

January Meeting (70–75 min.)

Status Report on EIR Teaching (5–10 min.)

I am always worried that students will forget some of what they have learned over the holiday, and I am always pleasantly surprised to see that they come back to school stronger than ever in terms of their reading abilities. Briefly report on successes you are seeing with your students—even after the holiday break!

Coaching for Comprehension (10 min.)

At the December meeting, I presented questions to help you focus on your questioning and coaching for comprehension and asked you to jot down notes on your practice related to these questions during the month. Refer back to these questions and discuss your progress with the group.

Discuss One-on-One Coaching, Status Report (5 min.)

Again, let me emphasize how important it is that this component of EIR be up and running. In December, I asked you to try to observe your one-on-one coaches and give them feedback. Discuss your issues and concerns.

Discuss Grade 2 Basic Procedures (20 min.)

In second grade, the focus after the first of the year is on students making the transition to independent reading. In February, second-grade teachers should come prepared to share their experiences with transition reading. Continue to work through Chapter 5, if you have not already done so. In particular, review and focus on Video 11 in which second-grade children are being coached in transition reading by their teacher. Discuss questions and concerns you have and brainstorm solutions.

Grade 2 Accelerated Procedures (20 min.)

If you have not done so, begin working on the grade 2 accelerated EIR process if you have students who would benefit from this as opposed to the grade 2 basic transition process. If there are parts of the grade 2 accelerated EIR routines that you wish to review, return to Chapter 6. Share questions and concerns and brainstorm solutions.

Many of the children in the accelerated program still need to work on their reading fluency. Often, they can decode, but they are slow. They also need to develop confidence in how to attack multisyllabic words; review this strategy in Chapter 5. (This strategy needs to be tied to the use of the advanced vowel chart in Figure 3-4.) I find it helpful to keep stressing that this strategy will only get students close to the real word. They need to think of a word that will make sense in the story as they are trying to sound out a word.

Video Viewing (15 min.)

Watch Video 12 to observe how the teacher coaches the children to think about the meaning of the story to help them decode. These students are engaged in transition reading.

Discuss the coaching you do to get children to think about meaning as they are decoding. Use examples from the video and from your students' success or lack of success at this point in time in using this strategy.

Video Sharing (15 min.)

Engage in video sharing. Also, fill out a new video-sharing sheet for February through April (refer to Figure 9-5).

Prepare for February Meeting (5 min.)

For the February meeting, one or two people per small group should bring in short video clips to share a predetermined piece of an EIR lesson.

February Meeting (60–80 min.)

Status Report on Children's Progress *(5–10 min.)*

I love February because by this time teachers are usually very excited about how their struggling readers are improving reading. I hope this is true for you, but if not, don't be discouraged. Your students are making progress! Very briefly, report on the successes you are seeing in your students.

Grade 2 Basic Procedures *(15 min.)*

Share ideas and concerns related to the transition phase.

A Note About Transition Reading

As I continue to work with teachers, we typically talk about how the transition phase of EIR with its focus on independent (cold) reading is harder than repeated reading for a number of reasons. Reading unfamiliar texts is more challenging for the students. They are not experiencing quite as much success as they did with the guided, repeated reading. (But they will get better, and this is what they need to be doing to become on-grade-level readers.) Also, it is harder to manage the other children when you are working with just two students at a time. Use independent activities similar to those listed on the lesson planners for exemplar transition books or the generic take-home activities all found on the DVD.

Many teachers have reported that they like the opportunity to work with just two children at a time. They say it allows them to understand a child's strengths and weaknesses. Discuss your successes and challenges with the use of the transition approach.

Review Procedures for Oral Reading Analysis

For students who are struggling with word recognition, get ready to begin oral reading analysis with them (see Chapter 5; also Taylor et al. 1995). In oral reading analysis, take three, 100-word samples of a student's reading of material at their instructional level (92 percent–97 percent accuracy in word recognition). Analyze these samples to determine one problem area on which to focus. Provide instruction in this focus area. As a student does subsequent oral readings, continue to assess in this focus area, monitoring with a progress chart to document the student's growth in the target area. Once a student has made good progress in one problem area, move to another as needed.

Grade 2 Accelerated Program *(15–30 min.)*

Remind the children why summarizing stories is important. You may tell them that they may need to summarize when they are telling their parents or a friend about a book or story they have read. The person they are talking to won't want to hear every detail about the story, so they need to be able to tell the main ideas in just a few sentences. Refer to the section of Chapter 6 on summarizing a story for help with modeling and coaching. Discuss the importance of releasing responsibility to the children when they are ready.

Video Sharing (15–30 min.)

Engage in video sharing.

Prepare for March Meeting (5 min.)

For the March meeting, one or two people per small group should bring in short video clips to share a predetermined piece of an EIR lesson. Try oral reading analysis and be prepared to talk about in March.

March Meeting (50–75 min.)

Status Report on Children's Progress (5–10 min.)

Briefly report on successes you are seeing with your students.

Grade 2 Basic Procedures (15-30 min.)

Using the Decoding Multisyllabic Words Strategy and the Advanced Vowel Chart

By now, you are probably working with your students on a strategy for attacking multisyllabic words. It is important to remind the children they can use this strategy when they are reading on their own and come to a long word they don't instantly recognize. This strategy works best if it is used on a word already in students' listening vocabulary, and many of the words struggling readers come across will, in fact, be words in their listening vocabulary. (See Chapter 5 for a strategy for decoding multisyllabic words.)

It doesn't matter if the children break a word into the exact syllables as found in the dictionary. Instead, they need to know that a chunk, or approximate syllable, has one vowel or vowel team per chunk. They need to learn to be flexible with their sounding out of syllables and blending syllables together. Give them a copy of the advanced vowel chart (see Figure 3-4 in Chapter 3 to help them remember the most common vowel sounds for a particular vowel or vowel team. If one sound doesn't work, try another.

Remind the children by sounding out words it will only get them close to the real word. As they are blending syllables together, they need to think of a word that is close to what they are saying and that would make sense in the story. I often find that children don't rely on context enough as they are sounding out multisyllabic words.

Conducting Oral Reading Analysis

Share experiences with oral reading analysis. Ask questions and get help fro colleagues on answering these questions. Discuss using data from oral reading analysis to target word-recognition instruction for individual students.

Grade 2 Accelerated Program

At this time in the year, you should be starting to use some of the informational books in your lessons if you haven't already done so. The written questions should elicit correct answers from the students and students should be able to read questions correctly, understand the questions, answer all parts of written questions, and answer in complete sentences. The questions also help students learn how to get their thoughts down on paper in a clear yet concise manner. Sometimes, children's written answers are either too general or too long or involved and unclear. As you use more challenging texts, the questions become more complex in terms of asking the children to summarize the most important ideas or getting them to explain processes or concepts they have read about.

Discuss children's strengths and weaknesses in answering written questions on the informational books. Brainstorm ways to help them with the problems they are having.

Video Sharing (15–30 min.)

Engage in video sharing.

Prepare for the April meeting (5 min.)

Before the next meeting, read the section on spring assessments in Chapter 7. At the April meeting, you should review the procedures and answer any questions members of the group may have.

April Meeting (50–65 min.)

Congratulations on all your hard work teaching EIR lessons this year! Your participation in the monthly meetings to work through the EIR professional learning sessions has, I hope, been a rewarding experience for you. I am sure your students have benefited greatly from your dedication. All children deserve the chance to learn to read well, and I commend you on your efforts to help your students make important progress in reading.

Status Report on Children's Progress (5–10 min.)

Briefly report on your students' successes

Discuss Grade-Level Procedures (20–25 min.)

Share your ideas and concerns. Discuss your successes, problems, and questions pertaining to the transition phase of the EIR program and to children's attempts at transition (independent) reading. Discuss plans for working with struggling readers in the next school year.

Assessments (25–30 min.)

Review the steps for completing the assessments in Chapter 7. Select the passages you will all use from an informal reading inventory. Typically, you should do the assessments during the first two weeks of May before things get really wild at the end of the school year.

Prepare for May Meeting (2 min.)

Be prepared to discuss your assessments and your overall reflections about the year, plus plans for next year.

May Meeting (50–65 min.)

Status of Children's Progress

Share your major successes. How many students will no longer need EIR? How many will require basic EIR next year?

Discuss Results of Assessments

Discuss how students did on the assessments and which assessments provided you with the most information. Were there any surprises (e.g., did some students whom you thought would do well—not do well? Did some students do much better than you expected?)?

Review Year and Discuss Plans for Next Year

Training One-on-One Coaches

One-on-one coaching is a very important component of EIR, but one that sometimes gets overlooked. It can be difficult to implement it if people are not readily available to read with the children every day. However, the children make greater progress in reading when they have a chance every day, or as close to every day as possible to practice reading their newest EIR story with a person who has been trained in how to coach, not tell them words in many instances, as they get stuck. In this one-on-one situation, children demonstrate to themselves their decoding abilities and don't have the pressure of another child sitting next to them calling out a word before they do.

Ceilia Huxley, the teacher we saw on the video and an EIR trainer, developed the material in this section. She has used it successfully with instructional aides and parent volunteers. The agenda that follows and handouts for participants for this one-hour session can be found in Figures 9-6 to 9-10. I hope it will help you get the one-on-one component going in your school.

The following is an agenda that provides training to volunteers, educational assistants, and older students who will be coaching EIR students as they read their EIR stories in a one-on-one situation.

To introduce EIR, first review the basic elements of the program as shown in Figure 9-7 below.

Coaching Training Agenda

1. Welcome and Introductions

2. What is EIR?

3. What is coaching?

4. Coaching Demonstration

5. Demonstrate Practice Coaching with a Volunteer

6. Participants Practice Coaching

7. Discuss Participants' Role in EIR

8. Tips

9. Follow-up Sessions

10. Questions, Concerns, Thoughts

Figure 9-6 Coaching Training Agenda

Basic Elements of EIR

▸ Twenty minutes of daily supplemental reading instruction to small groups of six or seven struggling readers

▸ All children receiving EIR participate in all of the regular reading instruction

▸ Three-day cycle reading and rereading a picture book and engaging in word-level activities, sentence writing, comprehension, and vocabulary related to the story

▸ Teacher concentrates on keeping children focused, on coaching them in their use of decoding and self-monitoring strategies, and on praising them for attempts at independence

▸ Teacher consistently monitors strategies as needed and helps children with reading and writing so they are successful

▸ Parent involvement is critical to students' success

Figure 9-7 Basic Elements of EIR

Independent Coaching Role

It is important to describe coaching. Have participants read through Figure 9-8. Coaching is giving children prompts, encouraging them, praising them as they attempt to figure out words on their own. They have been learning a number of different strategies to figure out unknown words as they come to them. The purpose of coaching is to help children learn to depend on themselves so they become good, independent readers. Review Figure 9-9, which lists prompts coaches can use as they are working with the children.

To illustrate coaching, show the following video clips:

▶ Video 3: Teacher working with two second-grade children in early December.

▶ Video 12: Teacher working with two second-grade children in early December.

Coaching Demonstration by Modeling, with Volunteer, and Through Partner Practice

As the presenter, model coaching by working through a story with future one-on-one coaches. Then, ask for a volunteer who will read another text as you coach. Finally, let people practice coaching with a partner using a third text.

Independent Coaching Role

▶ Work with one child at a time.

▶ Classroom teacher will give you the summary or book to use.

▶ Child will have a copy of the book.

▶ Assist child in reading the summary or book.

▶ Reinforce strategies.

▶ Give appropriate praise.

Figure 9-8 Independent Coaching Rule

Prompts for Teaching Children Decoding and Self-Monitoring Strategies

▶ Can you reread that? Did that make sense?

▶ You did a great job of figuring out that word. How did you do it?

▶ I like the way you self-corrected. How did you do that?

▶ Let's look at that word again. You said _____. Does that make sense (or look and sound right)?

Figure 9-9 Prompts for Teaching Children Decoding and Self-Monitoring Strategies

Figure 9-10 Tips for Working with Children

Return to Figure 9-8 to review the coach's role. Also, read through Figure 9-10 which provides tips for working with children. Ask group members to share questions, thoughts, and concerns. Schedule another session once the coaches have been working with children for four or five weeks.

Summary

I cannot stress enough the importance of the ongoing professional learning. Teachers have told me over the years that this monthly collegial reflection on their EIR instruction has helped them be more successful in teaching their students who need more support to become competent readers during the year.

It is my hope that this book and the forthcoming companion books for kindergarten, first, third, and fourth/fifth grades will help you and your school meet your struggling readers' needs. Should you have additional questions, go to the Heinemann website, www.heinemann.com, and look for additional resources on how to use EIR teaching routines and strategies. I think you will find that this intervention model is worth the time needed. When you understand and implement EIR in your classroom, you will feel tremendous pride in what your students will accomplish as they become successful, confident readers. Thank you for the important work you do with and for children.

Works Cited

Adams, M. J. 1990. *Beginning to Read: Thinking and Learning About Print.* Cambridge, MA: MIT Press.

Anderson, N. A. 2007. *What Should I Read Aloud?* Newark, DE: International Reading Association.

Au, K. H. 2006. *Multicultural Issues and Literacy Achievement.* Mahwah, NJ: Lawrence Erlbaum.

Bang, M. 1996 *Ten, Nine, Eight.* New York: Greenwillow.

Baumann, J. F., and E. J. Kame'enui. 2004. *Vocabulary Instruction: Research to Practice.* New York: Guilford.

Bear, D. R., M. Invernizzi, S. Templeton, and F. Johnston. 2007. *Words Their Way: Word Study for Phonics, Vocabulary, and Spelling Instruction.* 4th ed. Upper Saddle River, NJ: Pearson/Merrill Prentice Hall.

Beck, I. L., M. G. McKeown, and L. Kucan. 2002. *Bringing Words to Life: Robust Vocabulary Instruction.* New York: Guilford.

Blachowicz, C., and P. Fisher. 2000. "Vocabulary Instruction." In *Handbook of Reading Research, Vol. 3*, edited by M. L. Kamil, P. B. Mosenthal, P. D. Pearson, and R. Barr. Mahwah, NJ: Lawrence Erlbaum.

———. 2002. *Teaching Vocabulary in All Classrooms.* 2d ed. Upper Saddle River, NJ: Pearson/Merrill Prentice Hall.

Bohn, C. M., A. D. Roehrig, and M. Pressley. 2004. "The First Days of School in the Classrooms of Two More Effective and Four Less Effective Primary-Grades Teachers." *The Elementary School Journal* 104: 271–87.

Burningham, J. 1990. *Mr. Gumpy's Outing.* New York: Henry Holt.

Chorzempa, B. F., and S. Graham. 2006. "Primary-Grade Teachers' Use of Within-Class Ability Grouping in Reading." *Journal of Educational Psychology* 98: 529–41.

Christensen, C. A., and J. A. Bowey. 2005. "The Efficacy of Orthographic Rime, Grapheme-Phoneme Correspondence, and Implicit Phonics Approaches to Teaching Decoding Skills." *Scientific Studies of Reading* 9: 327–49.

Clay, M. 1993. *Reading Recovery: A Guidebook for Teachers in Training.* Portsmouth, NH: Heinemann.

Connor, C. M., F. J. Morrison, and L. E. Katch. 2004. "Beyond the Reading Wars: Exploring the Effect of Child-Instruction Interactions on Growth in Early Reading." *Scientific Studies of Reading* 8: 305–36.

Consortium for Responsible School Change. 2005. *Description of Common Findings Across Multiple Studies on School Change in Reading.* Minneapolis: University of Minnesota, Minnesota Center for Reading Research.

Cunningham, P. M. 2009. *Phonics They Use: Words for Reading and Writing.* 5th ed. Boston: Pearson.

Day, J. P., D. L. Spiegel, J. McLellan, and V. B. Brown. 2002. *Moving Forward with Literature Circles.* New York: Scholastic.

Dolezal, S. E., L. M. Welsh, M. Pressley, and M. M. Vincent. 2003. "How Nine Third-Grade Teachers Motivate Student Academic Engagement." *Elementary School Journal* 103: 239–67.

Duke, N. K., and V. S. Bennett-Armistead. 2003. *Reading and Writing Informational Text in the Primary Grades: Research-Based Practices.* New York: Scholastic.

Edwards, P. A. 2004. *Children's Literacy Development: Making It Happen Through School, Family, and Community Involvement.* Boston: Pearson/Allyn & Bacon.

Foorman, B. R., and J. Torgesen. 2001. "Critical Elements of Classroom and Small-Group Instruction Promote Reading Success in All Children." *Learning Disabilities Research and Practice* 16: 203–12.

Fountas, I. C., and G. S. Pinnell. 1996. *Guided Reading: Good First Teaching for All Children.* Portsmouth, NH: Heinemann.

Fuchs, L. S., D. Fuchs, M. K. Hosp, and J. R. Jenkins. 2001. "Oral Reading Fluency as an Indicator of Reading Competence: A Theoretical, Empirical, and Historical Analysis." *Scientific Studies of Reading* 5: 239–56.

Gaetz, T. M. 1991. "The Effects of a Self-Monitoring Checklist on Elementary Students' Post Reading Question-Answering Performance." Unpublished doctoral dissertation, University of Minnesota.

Galda, L., and B. Cullinan. 2010. *Literature on the Child.* 7th ed. Belmont, CA: Thomson/Wadsworth.

Gardiner, J. R. 1980. *Stone Fox.* New York: HarperCollins.

Graves, M. F. 2007. "Conceptual and Empirical Bases for Providing Struggling Readers with Multifaceted and Long-Term Vocabulary Instruction." In *Effective Instruction for Struggling Readers K–6,* edited by B. M. Taylor and J. E. Ysseldyke. New York: Teachers College Press.

Guthrie, J. T., A. Wigfield, and C. VonSecker. 2000. "Effects of Integrated Instruction on Motivation and Strategy Use in Reading." *Journal of Educational Psychology* 92: 331–41.

Guthrie, J. T., A. Wigfield, P. Barbosa, K. C. Perencevich, A. Taboada, M. H. Davis, et al. 2004. "Increasing Reading Comprehension and Engagement Through Concept-Oriented Reading Instruction." *Journal of Educational Psychology* 96: 403–23.

Hamre, B. K., and R. C. Pianta. 2005. "Can Instructional and Emotional Support in the First-Grade Classroom Make a Difference for Children at Risk of School Failure?" *Child Development* 76 (5): 949–67.

Hasbrouck, J., and G. A. Tindal. 2006. "Oral Reading Fluency Norms: A Valuable Assessment Tool for Reading Teachers." *The Reading Teacher* 59 (7): 636–44.

Heffernan, L. 2004. *Critical Literacy and Writer's Workshop.* Newark, DE: International Reading Association.

Hiebert, E. H., and B. M. Taylor. 2000. "Beginning Reading Instruction: Research on Early Interventions." In *Handbook of Reading Research, Volume III,* edited by M. L. Kamil, P. B. Mosenthal, P. D. Pearson, and R. Barr. Mahwah, NJ: Lawrence Erlbaum.

Hiebert, E. H., J. M. Colt, S. L. Catto, and E. C. Gury. 1992. "Reading and Writing of First-Grade Students in a Restructured Chapter I Program." *American Educational Research Journal* 29: 545–72.

Joyce, William. 1985. *George Shrinks.* New York: Harper Collins.

Juel, C., and C. Minden-Cupp. 2000. "Learning to Read Words: Linguistic Units and Instructional Strategies." *Reading Research Quarterly* 35: 458–92.

Kelley, M. J., and N. Clausen-Grace. 2007. *Comprehension Shouldn't Be Silent.* Newark, DE: International Reading Association.

Kletsien, S.B., and M. J. Dreher. 2005. *Informational Text in K–3 Classrooms: Helping Children Read and Write.* Newark, DE: International Reading Association.

Klingner, J. K., S. Vaughn, M. E. Arguelles, M. T. Hughes, and S. A. Leftwich. 2004. "Collaborative Strategic Reading: Real World Lessons from Classroom Teachers." *Remedial and Special Education* 25: 291–302.

Knapp, M. S. 1995. *Teaching for Meaning in High-Poverty Classrooms.* New York: Teachers College Press.

Krauss, Ruth. 1945. *The Carrot Seed.* New York: Harper and Row.

Kraus, Robert. 1989. *The Happy Day.* New York: Harper Collins.

Kuhn, M. R., and S. A. Stahl. 2003. "Fluency: A Review of Developmental and Remedial Practices." *Journal of Educational Psychology* 95: 3–21.

Leslie, L., and J. Caldwell. 2010. *Qualitative Reading Inventory 4.* New York: Longman.

Lipson, M. L., J. H. Mosenthal, J. Mekkelsen, and B. Russ. 2004. "Building Knowledge and Fashioning Success One School at a Time." *The Reading Teacher* 57 (6): 534–42.

Marshall, E. 1994. *Four on the Shore.* New York: Puffin.

Mathes, P. G., C. A. Denton, J. M. Fletcher, J. L. Anthony, D. J. Francis, and C. Schatschneider. 2005. "The Effects of Theoretically Different Instruction and Student Characteristics on the Skills of Struggling Readers." *Reading Research Quarterly* 40: 148–82.

Mazer, A. 1991. *The Salamander Room.* New York: Alfred A. Knopf, Inc.

National Reading Panel (NRP). 2000. *Teaching Children to Read: An Evidence-Based Assessment of the Scientific Research Literature on Reading and Its Implications for Reading Instruction.* Rockville, MD: National Institute for Child Health and Human Development, National Institutes of Health.

Oczkus, L. D. 2003. *Reciprocal Teaching at Work: Strategies for Improving Reading Comprehension*. Newark. DE: International Reading Association.

Olness, R. 2007. *Using Literature to Enhance Content Area Instruction: A Guide for K–5 Teachers*. Newark, DE: International Reading Association.

Palincsar, A., and A. Brown. 1986. "Interactive Teaching to Promote Independent Learning from Text." *The Reading Teacher* 39(8): 771–77.

Paratore, J. R., and R. L. McCormack, eds. 2007. *Classroom Literacy Assessment: Making Sense of What Students Know and Do*. New York: Guilford.

Pikulski, J. 1994. "Preventing Reading Failure: A Review of Five Effective Programs." *The Reading Teacher* 48: 30–39.

Pinnell, G., M. Fried, and R. Estice. 1990. "Reading Recovery: Learning How to Make a Difference." *The Reading Teacher* 90: 160–83.

Pressley, M. 2001. *Effective Beginning Reading Instruction: Executive Summary and Paper Commissioned by the National Reading Conference*. Chicago, IL: National Reading Conference.

Pressley, M. 2006. *Reading Instruction That Works: The Case for Balanced Teaching*. 3d ed. New York: Guilford.

Pressley, M., S. E. Dolezal, L. M. Raphael, L. Mohan, A. D. Roehrig, and K. Bogner. 2003. *Motivating Primary-Grade Students*. New York: Guilford.

Raphael, T. E., L. S. Pardo, and K. Highfield. 2002. *Book Club: A Literature-Based Curriculum*. 2d ed. Lawrence, MA: Small Planet.

Raphael, T. E., K. Highfield, and K. H. Au. 2006. *QAR Now*. New York: Scholastic.

Rasinski, T. V. 2003. *The Fluent Reader: Oral Reading Strategies for Building Word Recognition, Fluency, and Comprehension*. New York: Scholastic.

Rylant, C. 1985. *The Relatives Came*. New York: Bradbury Press.

Saunders, W. M., and C. Goldenberg. 1999. "Effects of Instructional Conversations and Literature Logs on Limited and Fluent English Proficient Students' Story Comprehension and Thematic Understanding." *The Elementary School Journal* 99: 279–301.

Simon, C. 1999. *Show and Tell Sam*. Danbury, CT: Children's Press.

Snow, C. E., M. S. Burns, and P. Griffin, eds. 1998. *Preventing Reading Difficulties in Young Children*. Washington, DC: National Academy.

Southall, M. 2009. *Differentiated Small-Group Reading Lessons*. New York: Scholastic.

Taberski, S. 2000. *On Solid Ground: Strategies for Teaching Reading K–3*. Portsmouth, NH: Heinemann.

Taylor, B. M. 1986. "Teaching Students How to Summarize Content Textbook Material." In *Teaching Main Idea Comprehension*, edited by J. Baumann. Newark, DE: International Reading Association.

Taylor, B. M. 1998. *A Brief Review of Research on the Learning to Read Process.* Minneapolis, MN: University of Minnesota.

Taylor, B. M. 2001. *The Early Intervention in Reading Program: Research and Development Spanning Twelve Years.* Boston: Houghton Mifflin.

Taylor, B. M. 2010a. *Catching Readers, Grade 1.* Portsmouth, NH: Heinemann.

————. 2010b. *Catching Readers, Grade 3.* Portsmouth, NH: Heinemann

————. 2010c. *Developing Successful, Engaged Readers K–8: A School-Based Professional Learning Model That Works.* Portsmouth, NH: Heinemann.

Taylor, M.B. forthcoming. *Catching Readers, Grades 4/5.* Portsmouth, NH: Heinemann.

Taylor, B. M., B. Hanson, K. J. Justice-Swanson, and S. Watts. 1997. "Helping Struggling Readers: Linking Small Group Intervention with Cross-Age Tutoring." *The Reading Teacher* 51: 196–209.

Taylor, B. M., L. Harris, P. D. Pearson, and G. E. Garcia. 1995. *Reading Difficulties: Instruction and Assessment.* 2d ed. New York: Random House.

Taylor, B. M., P. D. Pearson, D. S. Peterson, and M. C. Rodriguez. 2003. "Reading Growth in High-Poverty Classrooms: The Influence of Teacher Practices That Encourage Cognitive Engagement in Literacy Learning." *Elementary School Journal* 104: 3–28.

Taylor, B. M., P. D. Pearson, K. Clark, and S. Walpole. 2000. "Effective Schools and Accomplished Teachers: Lessons About Primary Grade Reading Instruction in Low-Income Schools." *Elementary School Journal* 101 (2): 121–66.

Taylor, B. M., D. S. Peterson, M. Marx, and M. Chein. 2007. "Scaling Up a Reading Reform in High-Poverty Elementary Schools." In *Effective Instruction for Struggling Readers, K–6*, edited by B. M. Taylor and J. E. Ysseldyke. New York: Teachers College Press.

Taylor, B. M., M. Pressley, and P. D. Pearson. 2002. "Research-Supported Characteristics of Teachers and Schools That Promote Reading Achievement." In *Teaching Reading: Effective Schools, Accomplished Teachers*, edited by B. M. Taylor and P. D. Pearson. Mahwah, NJ: Lawrence Erlbaum.

Taylor, B. M., R. Short, B. Frye, and B. Shearer. 1992. "Classroom Teachers Prevent Reading Failure Among Low-Achieving First-Grade Students." *The Reading Teacher* 45: 592–97.

Van den Branden, K. 2000. "Does Negotiation of Meaning Promote Reading Comprehension? A Study of Multilingual Primary School Classes." *Reading Research Quarterly* 35: 426–43.

Recommended Professional Readings

• •

Please note that this list is by no means exhaustive. However, I wanted to at least point you to books that I think will be useful for an individual or for groups of teachers to use together to learn new teaching techniques as part of a continual process of improving reading instruction.

Resources on Phonics and Word-Recognition Instruction

Bear, D. R., M. Invernizzi, S. Templeton, and F. Johnston. 2007. *Words Their Way: Word Study for Phonics, Vocabulary, and Spelling Instruction*. 4th ed. Upper Saddle River, NJ: Pearson/Merrill Prentice Hall.

Beck, I. 2006. *Making Sense of Phonics: The Hows and Whys.* New York: Guilford.

Cunningham, P. 2009. *Phonics They Use: Words for Reading and Writing.* 5th ed. Boston: Pearson.

Carnine, D. W., J. Silbert, E. J. Kame´enui, and S. G. Tarver. 2004. *Direct Instruction Reading.* 4th ed. Upper Saddle River, NJ: Pearson.

Gaskins, I. W., L. C. Ehri, C. Cress, C. O'Hara, and K. Donnelly. 1996. "Procedures for Word Learning: Making Discoveries About Words." *The Reading Teacher* 50: 312–27.

Resources on Fluency

Johns, J. L., and R. L. Berglund. 2005. *Fluency Strategies and Assessments.* Dubuque, IA: Kendall-Hunt.

Rasinski, T. V. 2000. "Speed Does Matter in Reading." *The Reading Teacher,* 54 (2): 146–51.

———. 2003. *The Fluent Reader: Oral Reading Strategies for Building Word Recognition, Fluency, and Comprehension.* New York: Scholastic.

Samuels, S. J., and A. Farstrup (eds.). 2006. *What Research Has to Say About Fluency Instruction,* 3rd ed. Newark, DE: International Reading Association.

Stahl, S. A., and M. R. Kuhn. 2002. "Making It Sound Like Language: Developing Fluency." *The Reading Teacher* 55 (6): 582–84.

Resources on Vocabulary

Bauman, J. F., and E. J. Kame´enui (Eds.). 2004. *Vocabulary Instruction: Research to Practice.* New York: Guilford.

Beck, I. L., and M. G. McKeown. 2002. "Text Talk: Capturing the Benefit of Read-Aloud Experience for Young Children." *The Reading Teacher* 55 (1): 10–20.

Beck, I., M. McKeown, and L. Kucan. 2002. *Bringing Words to Life: Robust Vocabulary Instruction.* New York: Guilford.

Blachowicz, C., and P. Fisher. 2002. *Teaching Vocabulary in All Classrooms.* 2d ed. Upper Saddle River, NJ: Pearson/Merrill Prentice Hall.

Graves, M. F. 2007. "Conceptual and Empirical Bases for Providing Struggling Readers with Multifaceted and Long-term Vocabulary Instruction." *Effective Instruction for Struggling Readers K–6,* edited by B. M. Taylor and J. E. Ysseldyke, 55–83. New York: Teachers College Press.

Resources on Comprehension Strategies

Block, C., and M. Pressley (Eds.). 2002. *Comprehension Strategies: Research-Based Practices.* New York: Guilford.

Duke, N. K., and V. S. Bennett-Armistead. 2003. *Reading and Writing Informational Text in the Primary Grades.* New York: Scholastic.

Kelley, M. J., and N. Clausen-Grace. 2007. *Comprehension Shouldn't Be Silent.* Newark, DE: International Reading Association.

Kletsien, S. B., and M. J. Dreher. 2005. *Informational Text in K–3 Classrooms: Helping Children Read and Write.* Newark, DE: International Reading Association.

Klingner, J. K., S. Vaughn, M. E. Arguelles, M. T. Hughes, and S. A. Leftwich. 2004. "Collaborative Strategic Reading: Real World Lessons from Classroom Teachers." *Remedial and Special Education* 25: 291–302.

Raphael, T. E., K. Highfield, and K. H. Au. 2006. *QAR Now.* New York: Scholastic.

Resources on Comprehension: High-Level Talk and Writing about Text

Anderson, N. A. 2007. *What Should I Read Aloud?* Newark, DE: International Reading Association.

Beck, I. L., and M. G. McKeown. 2002. "Text Talk: Capturing the Benefit of Read-Aloud Experience for Young Children." *The Reading Teacher* 55 (1): 10–20.

Cunningham, P. M., and D. R. Smith. 2008. *Beyond Retelling: Toward Higher Level Thinking and Big Ideas.* Newark DE: International Reading Association.

Day, J. P., D. L. Spiegel, J. McLellan, and V. B. Brown. 2002. *Moving Forward with Literature Circles.* New York: Scholastic

Galda, L., and B. Cullinan. 2010. *Literature on the Child.* 7th ed. Belmont, CA: Thomson/Wadsworth.

Kelley, M. J., and N. Clausen-Grace. 2007. *Comprehension Shouldn't Be Silent.* Newark, DE: International Reading Association.

Olness, R. 2007. *Using Lliterature to Enhance Content Area Instruction: A Guide for K–5 Teachers.* Newark, DE: International Reading Association.

Raphael, T. E., L. S. Pardo, and K. Highfield. 2002. *Book Club: A Literature-Based Curriculum.* 2d ed. Lawrence, MA: Small Planet.

Raphael, T. R., and S. McMahon. 1994. "Book Club: An Alternative Framework for Reading Instruction." *The Reading Teacher* 48 (2): 102–116.

Wood, K. D., N. L. Roser, and M. Martinez. 2001. "Collaborative Literacy: Lesson Learned from Literature." *The Reading Teacher* 55 (2): 102–111.

Resources on Balanced, Differentiated Instruction

Fountas, I. C., and G. S. Pinnell. 1996. *Guided Reading: Good First Teaching for All Children.* Portsmouth, NH: Heinemann.

Lapp, D., D. Fisher, and T. D. Wolsey. 2009. *Literacy Growth for Every Child: Differentiated Small-Group Instruction, K–6.* New York: Guilford.

Manning, M., G. Morrison, and D. Camp. 2009. *Creating the Best Literacy Block Ever.* New York: Scholastic.

Morrow, L. M. 2003. *Organizing and Managing the Language Arts Block: A Professional Development Guide.* New York: Guilford.

Pressley, M. 2006. *Reading Instruction That Works: The Case for Balanced Teaching.* 3d ed. New York: Guilford.

Routman, R. 2003. *Reading Essentials.* Portsmouth, NH: Heinemann.

———. 2008. *Teaching Essentials.* Portsmouth, NH: Heinemann.

Serravallo, J. 2010. *Reading Instruction in Small Groups.* Portsmouth, NH: Heinemann.

Southall, M. 2009. *Differentiated Small-Group Reading Lessons.* New York: Scholastic.

Taberski, S. 2000. *On Solid Ground: Strategies for Teaching Reading K–3.* Portsmouth, NH: Heinemann.

Walpole, S., and M. C. McKenna. 2009. *How to Plan Differentiated Reading Instruction: Resources for Grades K–3.* New York: Guilford.

Resources on Support for Struggling Readers

Fuchs, D., L. Fuchs, and S. Vaughn (Eds.). *Response to Intervention: An Overview for Educators*. Newark, DE: International Reading Association.

Gaskins, I. W. 2004. *Success with Struggling Readers: The Benchmark School Approach*. New York: Guilford.

McCormick, S. 2007. *Instructing Students Who Have Literacy Problems*. 5th ed. Upper Saddle River, NJ: Pearson.

Taylor, B.M. 2010.*Catching Readers, Grade 1*. Portsmouth, NH: Heinemann.

Taylor, B.M. 2010. *Catching Readers, Grade 2*. Portsmouth, NH: Heinemann.

Tyner, B. 2009. *Small-Group Reading Instruction: A Differentiated Teaching Model for Beginning and Struggling Readers*. Newark, DE: International Reading Association.

Tyner, B., and Green, S. E. 2005. *Small-Group Reading Instruction: A Differentiated Teaching Model for Intermediate Grade Readers, Grades 3–8*. Newark, DE: International Reading Association.

Vaughn, S., J. Wanzek, and J. M. Fletcher. 2007. "Multiple Tiers of Intervention: A Framework for Prevention and Identification of Students with Reading/ Learning Disabilities." In *Effective Instruction for Struggling Readers K–6*, edited by B. M. Taylor and J. E. Ysseldyke, 173–195). New York: Teachers College Press.

Resources on Motivating, Effective Pedagogy

Connor, C. M., F. J. Morrison, and L. E. Katch .2004. "Beyond the Reading Wars: Exploring the Effect of Child-Instruction Interactions on Growth in Early Reading." *Scientific Studies of Reading* 8: 305–36.

Kelley, M. J., and N. Clausen-Grace. 2007. *Comprehension Shouldn't Be Silent*. Newark, DE: International Reading Association.

Manning, M., G. Morrison, and D. Camp. 2009. *Creating the Best Literacy Block Ever*. New York: Scholastic.

Olness, R. 2007. *Using Literature to Enhance Content Area Instruction: A Guide for K–5 Teachers*. Newark, DE: International Reading Association.

Pressley, M. 2006. *Reading Instruction That Works: The Case for Balanced Teaching*. 3d ed. New York: Guilford.

Pressley, M., S. E. Dolezal, L. M. Raphael, L. Mohan, A. D. Roehrig, and K. Bogner. 2003. *Motivating Primary-Grade Students*. New York: Guilford.

Resources on Assessments

McKenna, M., and S. Stahl. 2003. *Assessment for Reading Instruction.* New York: Guilford.

Paratore, J. R., and R. L. McCormick (Eds.). 2007. *Classroom Reading Assessment: Making Sense of What Students Know and Do.* New York: Guilford.

Pressley, M. 2006. *Reading Instruction That Works: The Case for Balanced Teaching.* 3d ed. New York: Guilford.

Taberski, S. 2000. *On Solid Ground: Strategies for Teaching Reading K–3.* Portsmouth, NH: Heinemann.

Resources on Culturally Responsive Instruction

Au, K. 2006. *Multicultural Issues and Literacy Achievement.* Mahwah, NJ: Erlbaum.

Gaitan, C. D. 2006. *Building Culturally Responsive Classrooms: A Guide for K–6 Teachers.* Thousand Oaks, CA: Corwin.

For a list and review of books for teachers on English language learners, see Opitz, M. F., and J. L. Harding-DeKam. 2007. "Understanding and Teaching English-Language Learners." *The Reading Teacher* 60 (6): 590–93.

Resources on Schoolwide Reading Programs and Effective Schools

Allington, R. L., and S. A. Walmsley (Eds.). 2007. *No Quick Fix: Rethinking Literacy Programs in American's Elementary Schools* (RTI ed.). New York: Teachers College Press.

Lipson, M. L., J. H. Mosenthal, J. Mekkelsen, and B. Russ. 2004. "Building Knowledge and Fashioning Success One School at a Time." *The Reading Teacher* 57 (6): 534–42.

Morrow, L. M. 2003. *Organizing and Managing the Language Arts Block: A Professional Development Guide.* New York: Guilford.

Raphael, T., K. Au, and S. Goldman. 2009. "Whole School Instructional Improvement Through the Standards-Based Change Process." *Changing Literacies for Changing Times,* edited by J. Hoffman and Y. Goodman, 198–229. New York: Routledge Taylor Francis.

Resnick, L. B., and S. Hampton. 2009. *Reading and Writing Grade by Grade.* Revised edition. Newark, DE: International Reading Association.

Reyes, P., J. D. Scribner, and A. P. Scribner (Eds.). 1999. *Lessons from High-Performing Hispanic Schools.* New York: Teachers College.

Taylor, B. M., and P. D. Pearson (Eds.). 2002. *Teaching Reading: Effective Schools/Accomplished Teachers.* Mahwah, NJ: Erlbaum.

Taylor, B. M., P. D. Pearson, D. S. Peterson, and M. C. Rodriguez. 2005. "The CIERA School Change Framework: An Evidence-Based Approach to Professional Development and School Reading Improvement." *Reading Research Quarterly* 40 (1): 40–69.

Taylor, B. M., D. S. Peterson, M. Marx, and M. Chein. 2007. "Scaling Up a Reading Framework for Prevention and Identification of Students with Reading/Learning Disabilities." In *Effective Instruction for Struggling Readers K–6,* edited by B. M. Taylor and J. E. Ysseldyke, 216–234. New York: Teachers College Press.

Taylor, B. M., Raphael, T. E., and Au, H. H. (in press). "Reading and School Reform." *Handbook of Reading Research,* Volume IV., edited by M. L. Kamil, P. D. Pearson, P. Afflerbach, and E. Moje. London: Taylor & Francis.